ENVIRONMENTAL ACTION

Analyze Consider options Take action In Our Neighborhoods

HABITAT and Biodiversity

A Student Audit of Resource Use

STUDENT EDITION

E2: ENVIRONMENT & EDUCATION

DALE SEYMOUR PUBLICATIONS®
ORANGEBURG, NEW YORK

Developed by E2: Environment & Education™, an activity of the Tides Center.

Managing Editor: Cathy Anderson
Senior Editor: Jeri Hayes
Production/Manufacturing Director: Janet Yearian
Design Manager: Jeff Kelly
Senior Production Coordinator: Alan Noyes
Text and Cover Design: Lynda Banks Design
Art: Rachel Gage, Andrea Reider
Composition: Andrea Reider

This book is published by Dale Seymour Publications®,
an imprint of Addison Wesley Longman, Inc.

Dale Seymour Publications
125 Greenbush Road South
Orangeburg, NY 10962
Customer Service: 800 872-1100

Printed in the United States of America.

Printed on acid-free,
85% recycled paper
(15% post-consumer),
using soy-based ink.

ISBN 0-201-49533-3
DS36859
2 3 4 5 6 7 8 9 10–ML–01 00

CONTENTS

Welcome to Environmental ACTION!

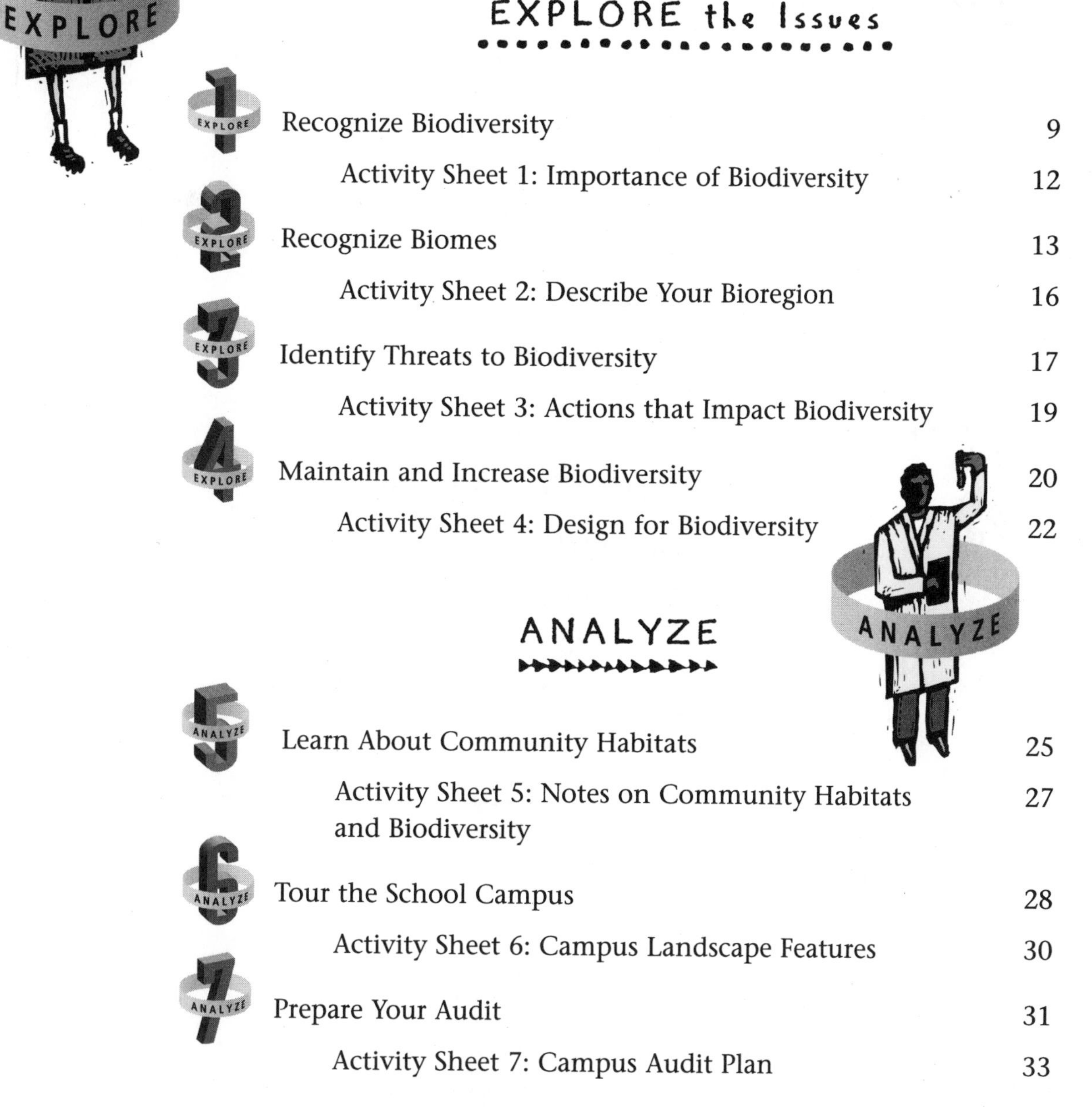

EXPLORE the Issues

1 Recognize Biodiversity 9
Activity Sheet 1: Importance of Biodiversity 12
2 Recognize Biomes 13
Activity Sheet 2: Describe Your Bioregion 16
3 Identify Threats to Biodiversity 17
Activity Sheet 3: Actions that Impact Biodiversity 19
4 Maintain and Increase Biodiversity 20
Activity Sheet 4: Design for Biodiversity 22

ANALYZE

5 Learn About Community Habitats 25
Activity Sheet 5: Notes on Community Habitats and Biodiversity 27
6 Tour the School Campus 28
Activity Sheet 6: Campus Landscape Features 30
7 Prepare Your Audit 31
Activity Sheet 7: Campus Audit Plan 33

Conduct Your Audit 34

Activity Sheet 8: Details of Study Area 36

Research Plant Species 37

Activity Sheet 9: Data Sheet for Landscape Plants 39

Summarize Findings 40

Activity Sheet 10: Campus Habitats 42

Act Locally 43

CONSIDER OPTIONS

Brainstorm Landscaping Ideas 47

Activity Sheet 11: Landscaping Options 49

Weigh the Costs and Benefits 50

Activity Sheet 12: Assess Costs and Benefits 52

Make Recommendations 53

Activity Sheet 13: Landscaping Proposal 55

Act Locally 56

TAKE ACTION

Choose Landscaping Measures	59
Activity Sheet 14: Rating Sheet	61

Prepare and Present Your Proposal	62
Activity Sheet 15: Proposal Checklist	64

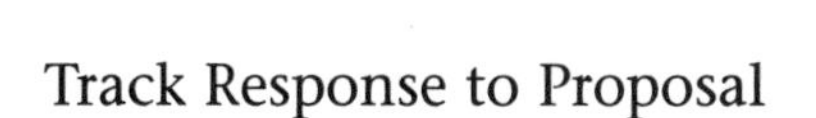

Track Response to Proposal	65
Activity Sheet 16: Tracking Sheet	67

Appendices

Issues and Information		69
Section A	Biodiversity	71
Section B	Biomes, Bioregions, and Habitats	74
Section C	Threats to Biodiversity	77
Section D	Conserving Biodiversity	79
Section E	Plants	83
Section F	Symbols to Use in Drawings of Landscape Plans	85
Section G	Principles of Sustainable Gardening and Landscaping	86
Section H	Tips for Planning and Maintaining a Sustainable Garden	88
Section I	Garden and Landscape Design	93
Section J	Organic Gardening	98
Glossary		102

Welcome to Environmental ACTION!

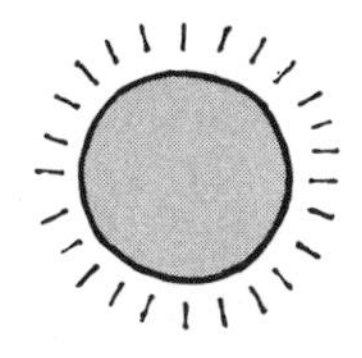

Welcome to Environmental ACTION!

This environmental program is designed to give you the knowledge and tools you need to make choices that will make a real difference to your quality of life, both now and in your future. You and all other living things modify the environment in order to live. What are the consequences of your actions on the food supply, atmosphere, and water cycle? The interrelationships of living things and long-term effects of actions are only beginning to be understood. As human beings, we are unique among earth's organisms because we can choose to change our daily behavior. We can change our actions to reduce our impact on the environment, improve our quality of life, and provide for the needs of future generations. We can conserve and preserve our natural resources.

Using your school as a laboratory, you will investigate environmental issues and analyze how they influence human health and the environment. Each module contains a set of ACT activities that will guide you in your investigations. ACT stands for

- Analyze
- Consider Options
- Take Action

What features does a lifestyle with a sustainable future have?

It is renewable. Resources are replaced as they are used.
It is balanced. People and systems work together to improve the environment in the present and to ensure the quality of life in the future.
It is manageable. Products are reusable, recyclable, and biodegradable.

Your Journal

Throughout the project, you will be using a Journal. It is a notebook in which you record all your observations and data, write down ideas, make sketches, and outline procedures.

You will need to use your Journal when you are conducting research in a study area, so it should be easy to carry. Your teacher may have specific instructions on what kind of notebook to use.

Action Groups

For most of the activities in this program, you spend part of your time working with a group of students. Your Action Group will work cooperatively, so that the group members benefit from each other's contributions. Sharing ideas, determining the best steps to take to achieve a goal, and dividing up tasks are just some of the advantages of working together.

Home activities can be done individually, but you may find that you prefer working with a group. Try to include your parents, brothers and sisters, or other family members in your work at home.

Topic Descriptions

The Environmental ACTION project that you are about to begin is divided into six modules, or units. Each module focuses on a different aspect of the environment. Your teacher may choose to do only one module, a few modules, or all of the modules. The modules cover the following topics:

Energy Conservation

Using the school as a research laboratory, you'll explore where energy comes from and how it is used, the effect of energy production on the environment, and how to improve energy efficiency at school and at home.

Food Choices

You will investigate the effects of food production, diet, and nutrition on human health and the environment. You will analyze your school's food service program and identify healthy choices and practices.

Habitat and Biodiversity

You will study the importance of biological diversity, landscape management, xeriscaping, composting, and integrated pest management (IPM). You'll tour the school grounds to assess the current landscaping lay-out and then evaluate the present condition in relation to environmental sustainability. This module also contains a step-by-step guide on how to create an organic garden and a seed bank.

Chemicals: Choosing Wisely

You will investigate the use of hazardous materials—paints, chemical products, cleaning supplies, pesticides—how they are stored and disposed of, and their potential effects on human health and the environment. After evaluating the results, you develop a plan for implementing the use of Earth- and human-friendly alternatives at school and home.

Waste Reduction

After you sort your school's garbage to identify recyclable and compostable materials and analyze the school's current waste practices, you will formulate a plan to reduce your consumption and waste at school and at home. Development or improvement of a recycling program may be part of the process.

Water Conservation

After an introduction to water consumption and water-quality issues, you'll conduct an audit of water usage and efficiency to determine whether current consumption practices on campus can be improved. You will then develop strategies for implementing water conservation at school and home.

Explore the Issues

RECOGNIZE BIODIVERSITY

Biodiversity is one of the most important characteristics of life on earth. It is as essential as the air we breathe and the water we drink. In order to ensure a healthy environment, biodiversity must be maintained. Find out how living things depend on each other and how changes in one species impact another.

> **THINK ABOUT IT**
>
> "Gardeners are emerging as principal biological heroes in the struggle of the era to maintain the biological diversity that sustains life on the planet. Backyard diversity is becoming prime territory for the conservation of life."
>
> —from *Seeds of Change 1994 Catalog,* Kenny Ausubel, ed., p. 55

Setting the Stage

Discuss these questions:

1. What is biodiversity?
2. Why is biodiversity important?

Vocabulary

- biodiversity
- ecosystem
- extinction
- genetic
- habitat
- interdependence
- species

Focus

A. Read the passage below and then discuss the questions. Additional background material is available in Issues and Information section A.

In any given habitat, living things depend on one another for survival. The bird needs the berry, the berry needs the bee, the bee needs the blossoms. If something happens to the blossoms, sooner or later the bird will be affected. Some changes in habitat can increase biodiversity. For example, adding plants to a landscape can

EXPLORE 1

attract a variety of insects, birds, and other wildlife. Other changes in habitat can decrease biodiversity. For example, damming a river, cutting down a forest, building a road, or clearing brush from a vacant lot can have a negative impact on the number and variety of living things found there. Upsetting the balance of living things in a given habitat can have far-reaching and sometimes irreversible consequences. In extreme cases of habitat change, biodiversity cannot be maintained and a species may be lost forever.

The graph below shows the number of species lost during this century. Loss of habitat is the reason for the sharp increase in species extinction. The only thing that will slow this rate of extinction is to restore habitats and increase biodiversity.

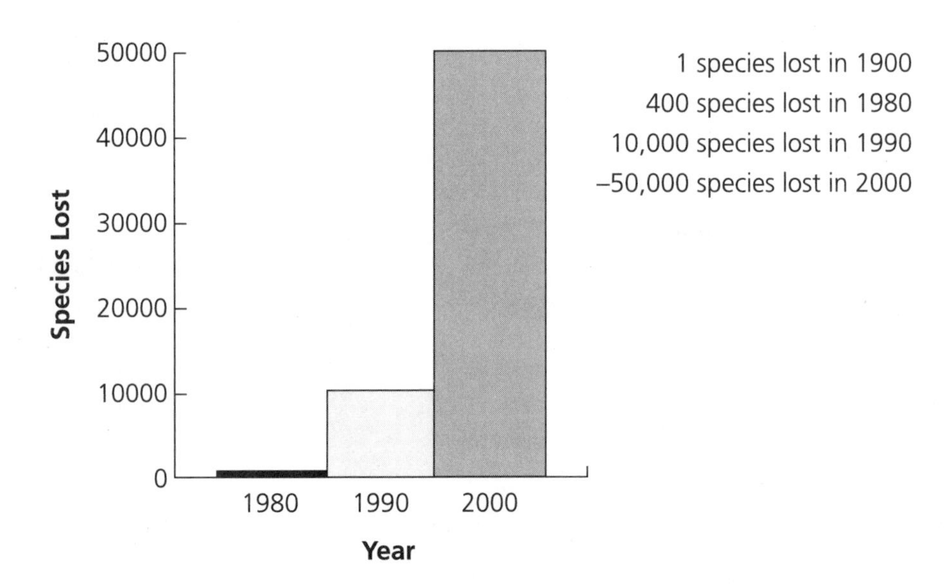

1. What do living things need in order to survive?
2. How do living things depend on each other?
3. What is an extreme result of habitat loss?

B. Complete all the work on Activity Sheet 1.

It's a Wrap

Share your responses to the questions on Activity Sheet 1. Then work as a class or in small groups to name as many plants and animals as you can think of in two minutes. Choose one person to list your ideas on the chalkboard. Look at the list and think about how the plants and

animals are interdependent. Identify as many connections as you can in two minutes. How does removing certain plants or animals from your list affect interdependence? What does this tell you about the importance of habitat and biodiversity?

Home

How do you depend on other species of plants and animals? During the next 24 hours, keep track of all the things you and your family use that are connected to another species. For example, furniture comes from trees, clothing comes from plants and animals, food comes from plants and animals. List your connections in your Journal.

Your teacher will give you a two-part activity sheet like the one below to use with this lesson.

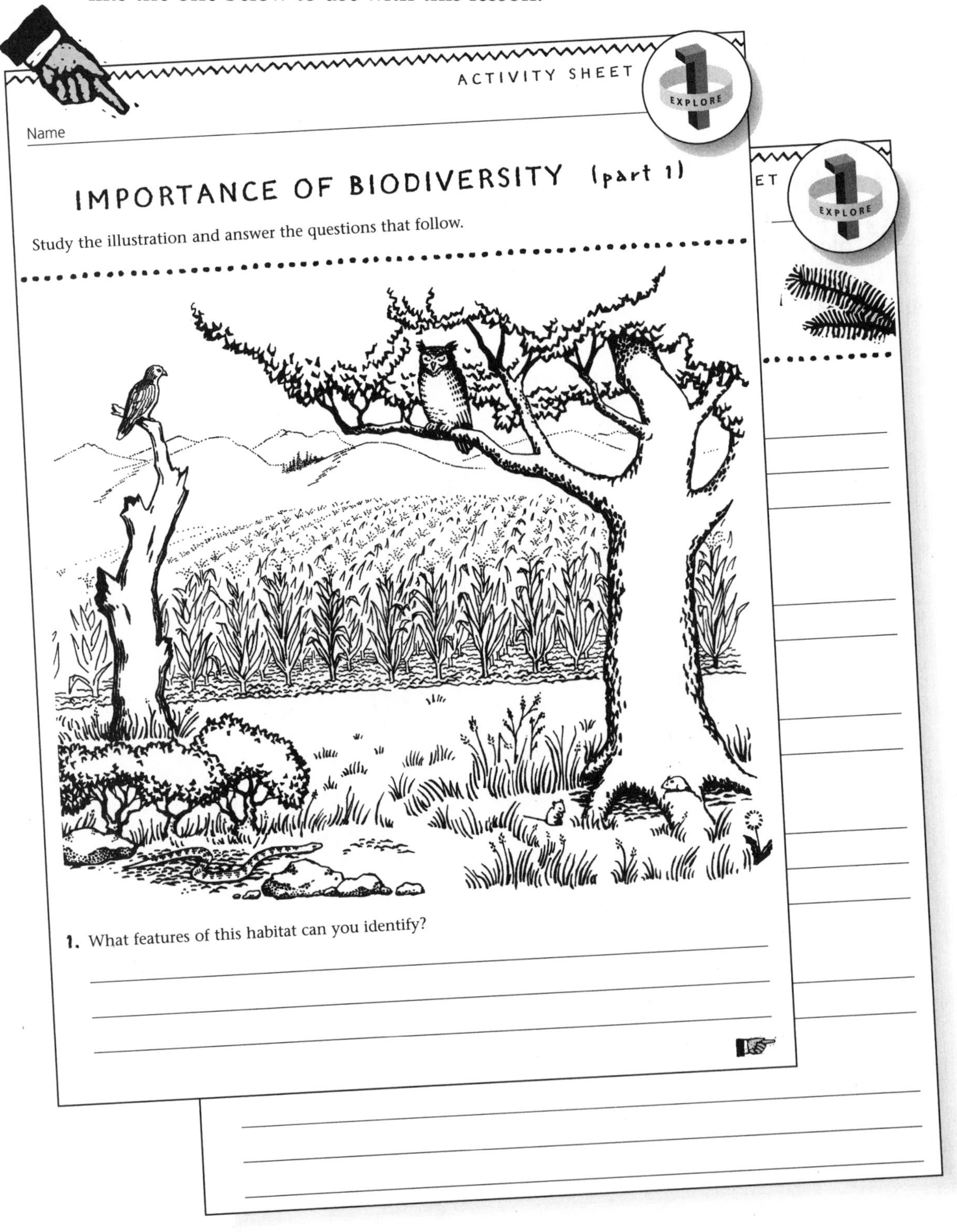

RECOGNIZE BIOMES

Regardless of the natural surroundings or the day-to-day conditions in any given place, plants and animals rely on their environment to provide them with the raw materials they need for life. Find out about the features that comprise the earth's biomes and how they affect biodiversity.

Setting the Stage

Discuss these questions:

1. What do living things need in order to survive?
2. What are some ways in which the basic needs of living things are provided for in your area?

Vocabulary

biome	precipitation
bioregion	savanna
chaparral	taiga
climate	temperate
coniferous	tropical
deciduous	tundra

Focus

A. The earth is divided into large ecosystems called biomes. Each biome is characterized by particular climate conditions, plant life, and animal life. Living things are adapted to survive even in biomes with extreme conditions, such as a desert or frozen tundra. The chart below gives you an overview of the earth's biomes. Use it to answer the questions. Additional background material is available in Issues and Information section B.

THINK ABOUT IT

"On the 27th of February I saw blackbirds and robin-redbreasts, and on the 7th of this month I heard the frogs....I hope you have and will continue to note every appearance, animal and vegetable, which indicates the approach of spring."

—excerpt of a letter from Thomas Jefferson to his daughter Maria, March 9, 1791; from *Thomas Jefferson's Garden Book 1766–1824*, annotated by Edwin Morris Betts, Philadelphia: The American Philosophical Society, 1944, p. 160

Biome	Climate	Common Plants	Common Animals
Tundra	very cold, dry; deep soil is permanently frozen; long, dark winters	few species; lichens, mosses, low shrubs	wolves, lemmings, polar bears, Arctic foxes, migratory birds; most migrate long distances
Taiga	cold winters, short growing season	evergreen shrubs and coniferous trees (fir, spruce, pine); some deciduous trees (birch, aspen)	bears, moose, wolves, ducks, loons, migratory birds
Temperate Coniferous Forest	damp, cool mountain slopes; coastal areas with mild winters and heavy rains	coniferous evergreen trees (redwood, cedar, hemlock, pine)	bears, elk, wolves, mountain lions
Temperate Deciduous Forest	cold to mild winters, long growing season, warm summers, high rainfall	many species; deciduous hardwood trees dominate (elm, maple, oak)	raccoons, squirrels, deer, many different birds
Chaparral	rainy, mild winters; hot, dry summers	low shrubs with small leaves (scrub oak, manzanita)	mule deer, coyotes, many lizards and birds
Desert	extremely dry; little or no rainfall	cacti, euphorbias, small-leafed or fleshy plants able to withstand heat and drought	small rodents, snakes, lizards, birds
Grassland	sparse or intermittent rainfall, temperate	huge, treeless areas covered by grasses	wolves, bison, pronghorns, coyotes, antelope, buffalo
Savanna	long dry season	grasses and a few trees (baobab, acacia)	giraffes, lions, zebras, jackals
Tropical Rain Forest	high rainfall, warm temperatures year-round	many different species; broadleaf evergreen trees, palms, tree ferns, climbing vines	many different species; bats, birds, lizards, snakes, monkeys

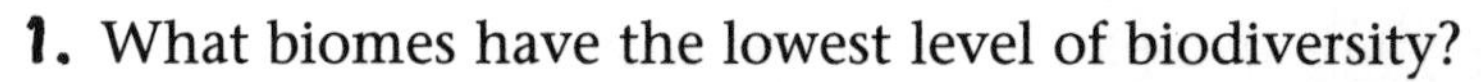

1. What biomes have the lowest level of biodiversity?
2. How might a short growing season affect animal life?
3. What adaptations can you identify for living things in biomes with extreme climate conditions?
4. What features characterize the biome with the highest level of biodiversity?
5. What biome do you live in?

B. Complete all the work on Activity Sheet 2.

It's a Wrap

Share the observations you made on Activity Sheet 2. Then write a paragraph to compare two different biomes or describe how biomes change the closer you get to the equator.

Home

In your Journal, list the plants and animals that you observe around your home, neighborhood, or community. Use a field guide and Issues and Information section E to help you. Write descriptions for animals or plants that you cannot yet name. Decide which animals or plants are native to your area. Which have special adaptations that enable them to survive in your bioregion?

Your teacher will give you a two-part activity sheet like the one below to use with this lesson.

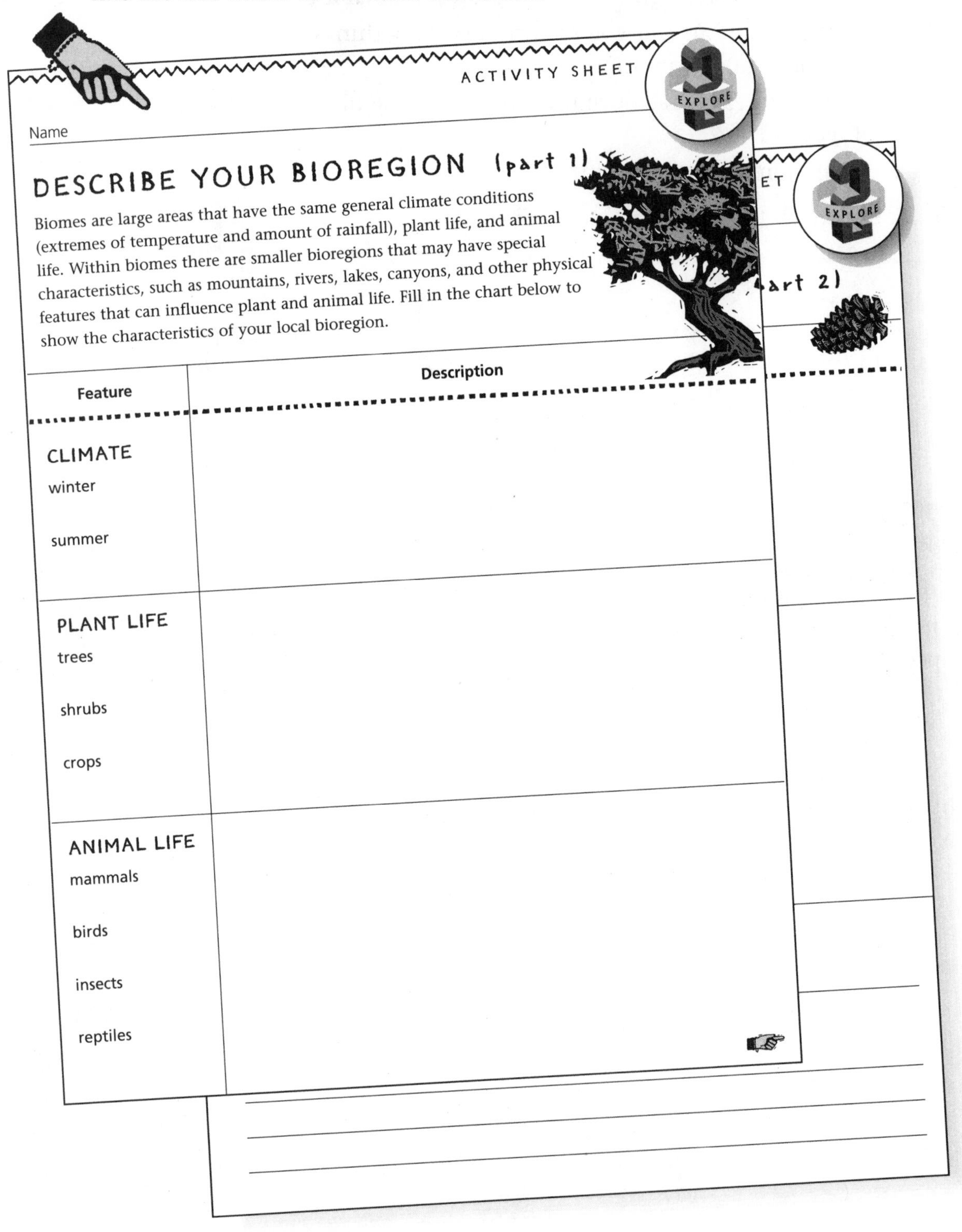
ACTIVITY SHEET

EXPLORE

Name

DESCRIBE YOUR BIOREGION (part 1)

Biomes are large areas that have the same general climate conditions (extremes of temperature and amount of rainfall), plant life, and animal life. Within biomes there are smaller bioregions that may have special characteristics, such as mountains, rivers, lakes, canyons, and other physical features that can influence plant and animal life. Fill in the chart below to show the characteristics of your local bioregion.

Feature	Description
CLIMATE winter summer	
PLANT LIFE trees shrubs crops	
ANIMAL LIFE mammals birds insects reptiles	

IDENTIFY THREATS TO BIODIVERSITY

The interdependence of living things creates a complex web, and like a web, once the delicate connections are broken, they can be difficult or even impossible to repair. Find out about the factors that threaten biodiversity and what can be done to maintain or increase biodiversity.

Setting the Stage

Discuss these questions:

1. What human activities threaten biodiversity?
2. What can be done to maintain or increase biodiversity?

Vocabulary

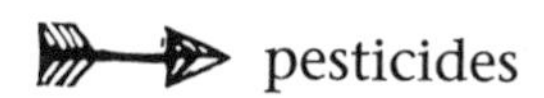 pesticides

Focus

A. The chart below lists factors that threaten biodiversity around the world. Some of them are caused by natural occurrences, and some are caused by people. Some have global consequences, and some affect only a small, localized population. Study the chart and use the information to answer the questions. You may wish to read more about the consequences of habitat destruction in Issues and Information section C.

1. What are some examples of natural disasters that can threaten biodiversity?
2. What are some examples of human-caused habitat destruction?
3. How does habitat destruction threaten biodiversity?
4. What are some examples of how resources are exploited?

THINK ABOUT IT

"DDT endures in the earth where we spread it once, and rises from the earth in blackfly livers that the whippoorwill eats."

—from *Seasons at Eagle Pond* by Donald Hall, New York: Ticknor & Fields, 1987, p. 45

Natural Factors	Human-Caused Factors
disease	habitat destruction
changes in climate	pollution
natural disasters	use of pesticides
competition between species	exploitation of resources
	introduction of nonnative species

5. How does this threaten biodiversity?
6. How do all of the factors in the chart relate to habitat destruction?

B. Complete all the work on Activity Sheet 3.

It's a Wrap

Share your responses to the questions on Activity Sheet 3. Then work in pairs or in small groups to plan a campaign to maintain or increase biodiversity in your bioregion. Make a poster, tape a public service announcement, or write a jingle to kick off your campaign.

Home

Use your Journal to make a list of activities you have observed at home or at school or in your community that might contribute to habitat destruction and impact biodiversity. Make another list of activities you have observed that enhance habitats and help to maintain biodiversity.

Your teacher will give you a two-part activity sheet like the one below to use with this lesson.

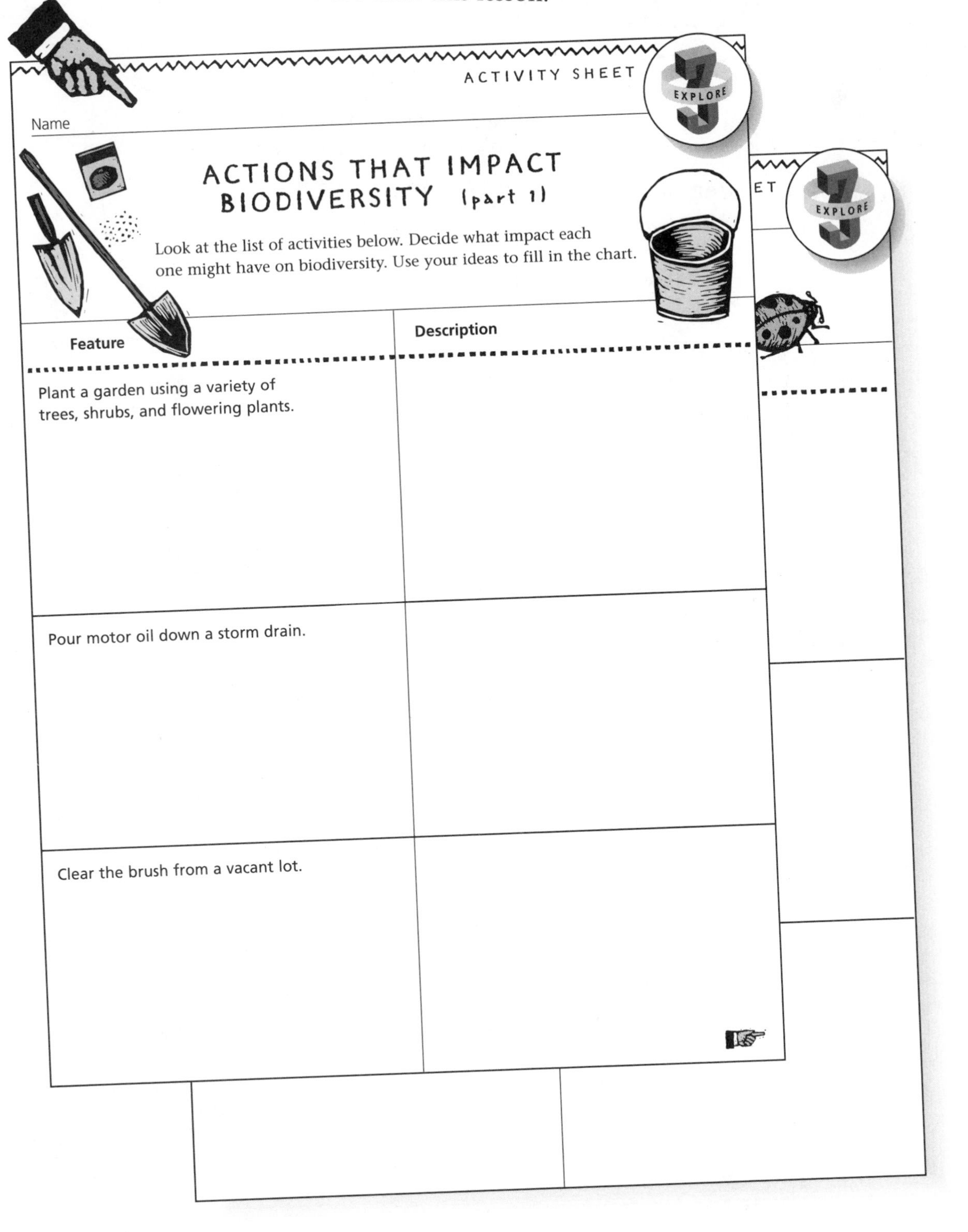

ACTIVITY SHEET

Name

ACTIONS THAT IMPACT BIODIVERSITY (part 1)

Look at the list of activities below. Decide what impact each one might have on biodiversity. Use your ideas to fill in the chart.

Feature	Description
Plant a garden using a variety of trees, shrubs, and flowering plants.	
Pour motor oil down a storm drain.	
Clear the brush from a vacant lot.	

MAINTAIN AND INCREASE BIODIVERSITY

Helping to maintain or increase biodiversity can begin in your own back yard. Find out about how landscaping can be used to attract and provide for insects, birds, and animals.

Setting the Stage

Discuss these questions:

1. How can gardens or landscaping help to maintain or increase biodiversity?
2. What landscaping features can help to increase biodiversity?

Vocabulary

irrigation
landscaping
topsoil

Focus

A. Study the list of landscaping practices. Additional material on creating sustainable landscapes can be found in Issues and Information section G.

1. Plant trees and groundcovers that help conserve water, create shade, and provide wind protection.
2. Install a drip irrigation system to conserve water and protect topsoil.
3. Avoid use of chemical pesticides and fertilizers.
4. Compost garden waste.
5. Install a water source, such as a birdbath, fountain, or pond.
6. Use plants that produce flowers, berries, seeds, nuts.
7. Add ladybugs to the garden.

THINK ABOUT IT

"The marigold is a cure-all in the garden. It exudes a substance that kills off bugs and whitefly, making it an ideal companion plant for just about everything."

—from *The Country Diary of Garden Lore* by Julia Jones and Barbara Deer, New York: Summit Books, 1989, p. 89

Think about how each of the landscaping practices might help to maintain or increase biodiversity. Use the list to answer the following questions.

1. Which of these practices will help provide shelter for birds and other wildlife?
2. Which of these practices will provide water for plants and animals?
3. Which of these practices will provide food?
4. How do some of these practices help the environment?
5. What other ways can these practices help to maintain or increase biodiversity?

B. Complete Activity Sheet 4. Symbols that you may want to use in your drawing can be found in Issues and Information section F. Plant lists can be found in Issues and Information section E.

It's a Wrap

Share your landscape features from Activity Sheet 4 with your classmates. Then identify three ways that landscaping can be used to maintain biodiversity and three ways that it can be used to increase biodiversity.

Home

Investigate your own back yard or a nearby park. Use your Journal to record your ideas for maintaining or increasing biodiversity in these places. Add to your plant list as you explore the area.

Your teacher will give you an activity sheet like the one below to use with this lesson.

ACTIVITY SHEET

Name

DESIGN FOR BIODIVERSITY

In the space below, sketch a plan for a park, greenspace, campus, city, or back yard that is designed to maintain or increase biodiversity. Think about what you have learned about landscaping practices and then put your imagination to work.

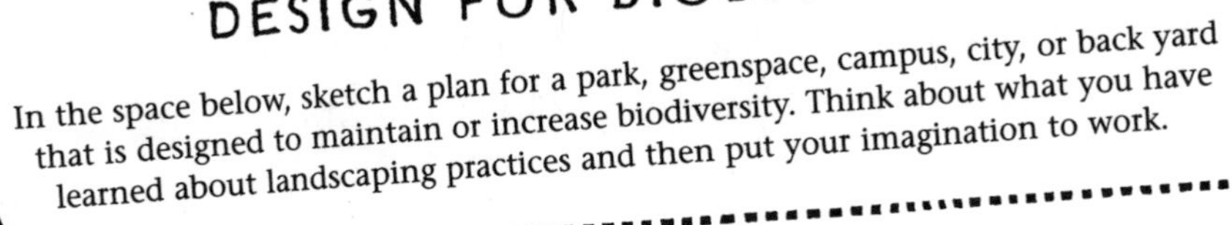

Analyze

LEARN ABOUT COMMUNITY HABITATS

A resource person from the community will come to your class to talk about local habitats and biodiversity. Use this opportunity to obtain as much specific information as you can about biodiversity in your area and what your community does to support plant and animal life.

Setting the Stage

Discuss these questions:

1. How are habitats and biodiversity supported within the community?
2. How can habitats and biodiversity within the community be improved?

Focus

As you learn about habitats and biodiversity in your community, use Activity Sheet 5 as a guide for asking questions. The information provided by the resource person will help you fill in the chart.

Think about the landscape around your community. How did it look in its natural state, before houses and roads were built on it? Where in your community can you still find places that show what the landscape used to be like? How has community planning preserved the natural environment? How does the natural environment affect all living things in the community?

It's a Wrap

Discuss your work on Activity Sheet 5 with your classmates. In your Journal, write a short paragraph telling how the guest speaker helped you learn more about habitats and biodiversity in your community.

THINK ABOUT IT

"In a much larger context, children who develop an affinity for nature and living things and who have a direct personal connection with the world outside are more likely to grow up honoring, respecting and protecting the environment—working for and with it, not against it."

—from "Growing Up in the Garden" by Linda Estrin in *The Southern California Gardener*, Volume 4, Number 3, January–February 1995, p. 1

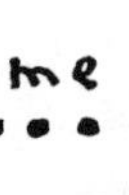

Home

You have explored biomes and bioregions. Now it is time to investigate an even smaller part of your bioregion. What kinds of habitats are found near your home? What kinds of plants and animals live there? Write a description in your Journal.

Your teacher will give you a two-part activity sheet like the one below to use with this lesson.

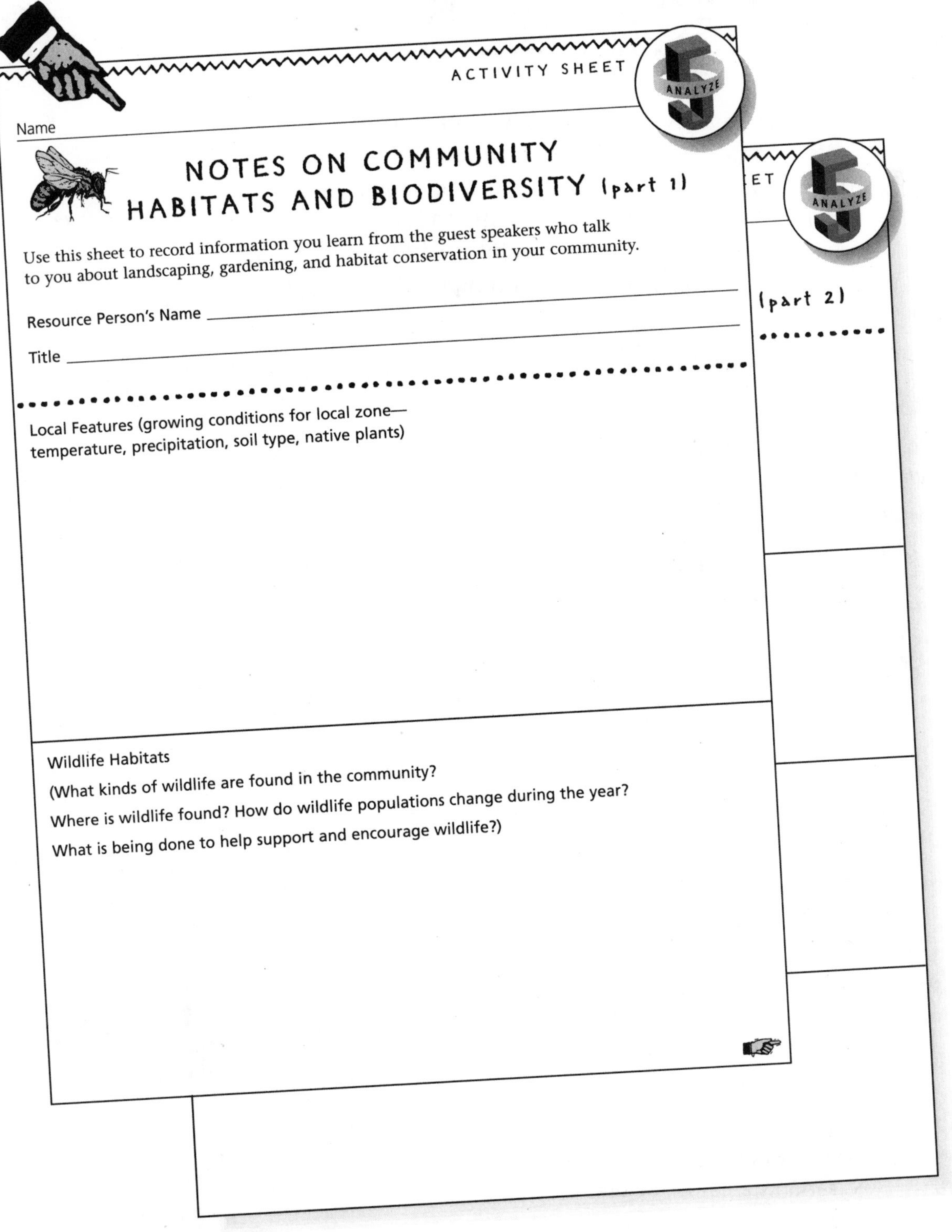
ACTIVITY SHEET

ANALYZE 5

Name

NOTES ON COMMUNITY HABITATS AND BIODIVERSITY (part 1)

Use this sheet to record information you learn from the guest speakers who talk to you about landscaping, gardening, and habitat conservation in your community.

Resource Person's Name

Title

Local Features (growing conditions for local zone—temperature, precipitation, soil type, native plants)

Wildlife Habitats
(What kinds of wildlife are found in the community?
Where is wildlife found? How do wildlife populations change during the year?
What is being done to help support and encourage wildlife?)

TOUR THE SCHOOL CAMPUS

A school resource person will come to your class to talk about garden and landscaping practices on campus. You will then take a tour of the school campus to find out where different kinds of trees and plants are located. You will use this information to draw a rough sketch of landscape features on campus.

Setting the Stage

Discuss these questions:

1. What kinds of habitats are found on the school campus?
2. How can landscaping affect biodiversity?

Focus

Use this opportunity to obtain specific information about school habitat and biodiversity issues. Think of at least three questions that you want to ask the resource person. Record your questions in your Journal. Topics for questions include the following:

1. how the school grounds relate to features of the local bioregion
2. the landscape features of the campus when it was in its natural state
3. the school's trees and plants (types and requirements)
4. maintenance of the school's trees and plants (water, pesticides/herbicides, soil conditioning, fertilizer, personnel)

The resource person will take you on a campus tour to show you the main landscape and garden features. Use Activity Sheet 6 as a guide for taking notes and

THINK ABOUT IT

"Plants scrub pollutants from the air. One tree can remove 26 pounds of carbon dioxide from our atmosphere each year, which is the same amount emitted by one car every 11,000 miles."

—from *Greening the Urban Ecosystem*, National Arbor Day Foundation and California Association of Nurserymen, p. 3

sketching locations of trees and plants on the school grounds. When you return to class, fill in as many details as you can.

Symbols to use for landscape features can be found in Issues and Information section F.

It's a Wrap

Discuss your work on Activity Sheet 6 with your classmates. What surprised you most about the tour? In your Journal, write a short paragraph telling how the guest speaker helped you learn more about the school's landscape features and needs.

Home

What did the landscape around your home look like before your neighborhood was built? Write a description in your Journal.

Your teacher will give you an activity sheet like the one below to use with this lesson.

ACTIVITY SHEET

Name

CAMPUS LANDSCAPE FEATURES

In the space below, make a rough sketch of the school campus. Include locations of buildings, parking lots, trees, shrubs, gardens, lawns, and other features that you notice during the campus tour. Include details learned from the guest speaker. Make a key for the symbols you use.

Rough Sketch of Campus Landscape Features

Key—Symbols Used in Sketch

PREPARE YOUR AUDIT

Using your sketch and campus tour notes, you will divide the campus into study area sites for the audit.

Setting the Stage

Discuss these questions:

1. What are the main areas where plants are located on the school campus?
2. What features of biodiversity does each region have?
3. How will you audit campus habitats?

Focus

A. With your class, plan a strategy for auditing campus habitats, identifying features of biodiversity, and evaluating landscape practices. Use the information you collected in the previous activities to divide the campus into study areas.

B. Organize the different parts of campus into research sites that can be assigned to Action Groups for the audit. You might divide the areas by use—recreation, leisure, traffic—or by type of vegetation—groundcover, field, lawn—or by location—playing field, parking area, front entrance, courtyard.

C. Meet with your Action Group. Use Activity Sheet 7 to record the decisions you make about how your audit will be organized. Find out whether you will need permission to conduct your audit. Are there areas closed to students? Do you need permission to be in certain areas during regular class time?

THINK ABOUT IT

"Surround yourself with nature and let it breathe life into your soul."

—from *Inneractions* by Stephen C. Paul, p. 43. Copyright ©1992 by Stephen C. Paul. Reprinted by permission of HarperCollins Publishers, Inc.

It's a Wrap

In your Journal, list the school habitats that require the most maintenance and which have the most wildlife. Discuss with your classmates how well your audit plan has covered these important sites.

Home

Take a walk around your home. In your Journal, draw a sketch of the buildings, boundaries, and landscaping on your lot.

Your teacher will give you a two-part activity sheet like the one below to use with this lesson.

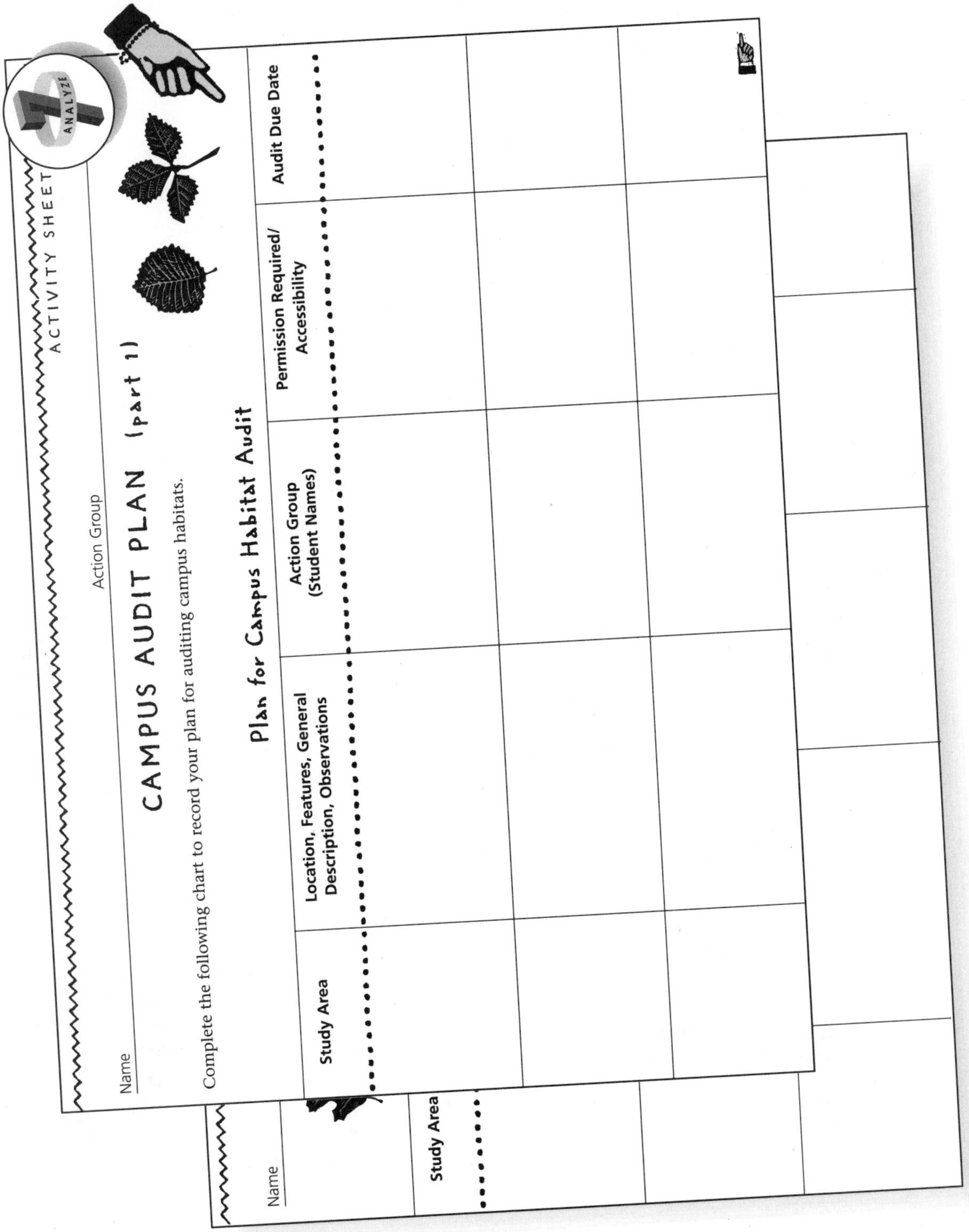

ANALYZE

ACTIVITY SHEET

Name

Action Group

CAMPUS AUDIT PLAN (part 1)

Complete the following chart to record your plan for auditing campus habitats.

Plan for Campus Habitat Audit

Study Area	Location, Features, General Description, Observations	Action Group (Student Names)	Permission Required/ Accessibility	Audit Due Date

Name

Study Area

CONDUCT YOUR AUDIT

Your Action Group will inspect its study area to create a detailed diagram of the site.

Setting the Stage

Discuss these questions:

1. What are the features of the habitat in my study area?
2. What factors affect the biodiversity of my study area?

Focus

A. Working with your Action Group, evaluate your site by compiling a detailed description of it to use in creating an accurate diagram. Include all of the existing plants (see Issues and Information section F for symbols) and slopes and hills that affect drainage. Select one member of your group to record your findings.

B. Discuss ways for your group to find out about the plants and animals that are found at your site. Field guides and local resources can help you as you create a detailed map of your study area. You will need to find out about how the landscaping at your site is maintained and assess parts of the site that might pose difficulties, such as deep shade, low-lying places where water collects, heavy traffic areas. Then you will determine cost-effective measures for enhancing the area.

C. Divide up responsibilities among members of your group. Will everyone work together, or will you split up and work individually or in pairs? If you split up, how will you divide up the site? For example, will some of you focus on plants, some on animals, and some on maintenance practices?

THINK ABOUT IT

"Roses become compost; compost feeds the garden for the growth of new roses."

—from *Buddha's Little Instruction Book* by Jack Kornfield, p. 98

It's a Wrap

In your Action Group, review your work on Activity Sheet 8 and the detailed map of your study area. Write three things that you learned about your study area and three things that you want to do to increase your knowledge of your study area.

Home

Select a natural area that is not actively maintained, such as a back yard, a vacant lot, or a roadway. In your Journal, write your observations about the features of the area.

Your teacher will give you a two-part activity sheet like the one below to use with this lesson.

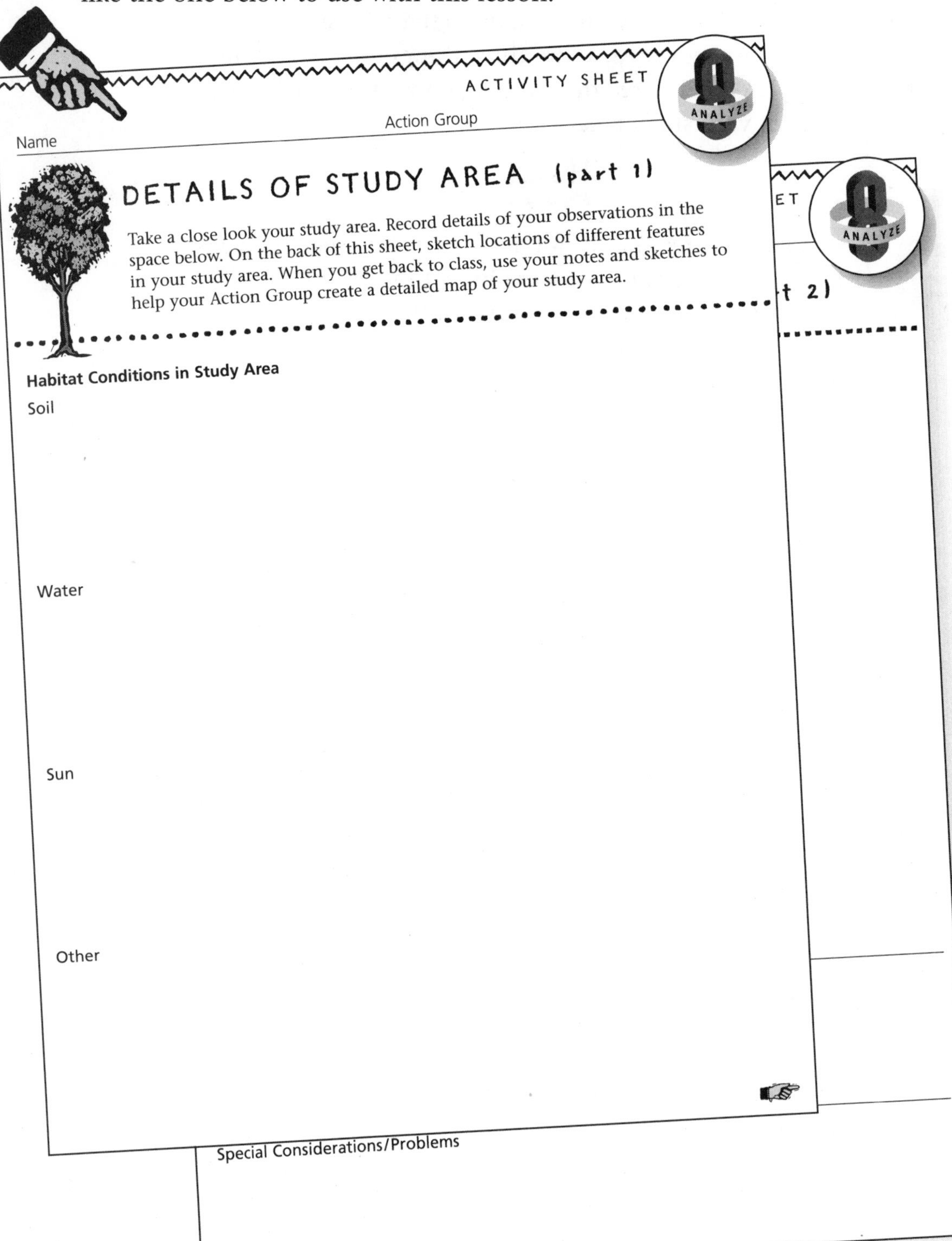
ACTIVITY SHEET

Name

Action Group

DETAILS OF STUDY AREA (part 1)

Take a close look your study area. Record details of your observations in the space below. On the back of this sheet, sketch locations of different features in your study area. When you get back to class, use your notes and sketches to help your Action Group create a detailed map of your study area.

Habitat Conditions in Study Area

Soil

Water

Sun

Other

RESEARCH PLANT SPECIES

Now that you've identified the features of the habitat and biodiversity of your study area, find out more about the site and how it is maintained.

Setting the Stage

Discuss these questions:

1. In researching plants in your study area, what kinds of information will be useful to you?
2. How will you find the information you need?

Focus

Meet with your Action Group. Give each item on the landscape map a number and name if possible. Also include the approximate number of each variety of plant. For example:

1. azalea [12]
2. oak tree [1]
3. flowering groundcover (unknown) [32 square feet]

If your group is working from more than one map, put together a list for each. Individual or pairs of group members can choose an item on the list for further research. Use Activity Sheet 9 to help you organize your data. Be sure to include the following information:

1. species name
2. approximate number
3. climate, soil, and water requirements
4. distinguishing features (color, smell, proportion, seasonal changes)
5. maintenance considerations (water requirements, ongoing care, need for pesticides/herbicides)

THINK ABOUT IT

"The plow brought death to the natural prairie....An acre of tall-grass...once harbored as many as three hundred kind of grasses and wildflowers."

—from *Three Faces of Eden* by Stanwyn G. Shelter, p. 231

Think about where you are going to find the information you need. Library reference books, periodicals, and local nurseries can provide resources. At the bottom of Activity Sheet 9, record the resources you used.

It's a Wrap

After the Action Groups have completed their research, a representative from each group should summarize the group's findings for the rest of the class. If students had trouble finding information, classmates may be able to suggest helpful resources and strategies.

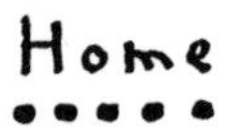

Identify three plants that grow around your home, research each of them, and record the information in your Journal.

Your teacher will give you an activity sheet like the one below to use with this lesson.

Name

DATA SHEET FOR LANDSCAPE PLANTS

Use the following chart to collect information about the plants in your assigned area. Use a separate sheet for each different species of plant.

Study Area	Plant #
Species Name	
Approximate Number of Plants	
Preferences/Requirements • Climate • Soil • Water • Other	
Distinguishing Features	
Maintenance Considerations • Watering • Ongoing Care • Pesticides/Herbicides • Other	
Information Sources	

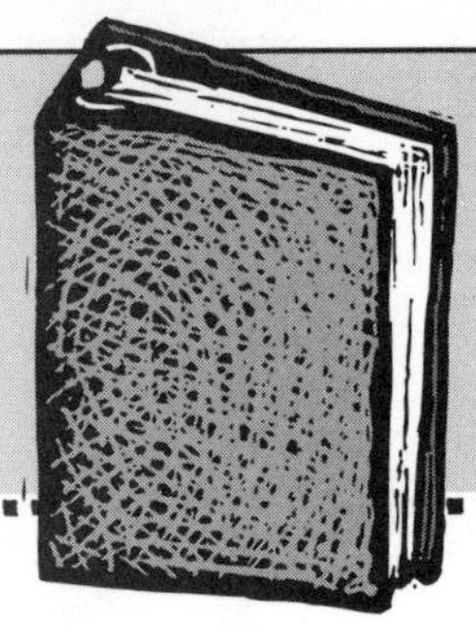

SUMMARIZE FINDINGS

During this activity, you will review the results of your audit and evaluate how habitats are maintained and biodiversity is supported at your site. Then you will write a summary of your findings.

Setting the Stage

Discuss these questions:

1. How are habitats maintained at your study area?
2. How is biodiversity supported at your study area?
3. What problems are associated with the habitat at your study area?

Focus

A. Meet with the entire class to discuss and combine the information gathered by all of the Action Groups. Include the following in your group's report:

1. landscaping in your group's study area
2. landscaping practices that enhance the habitat or encourage biodiversity
3. problems such as bad drainage, high traffic, reliance on pesticides and herbicides, labor-intensive maintenance, high water consumption, poor soil
4. any other observations about how biodiversity is affected at the site

Record information from the class discussion on Activity Sheet 10.

B. Meet with your Action Group to discuss and compare the landscaping practices that enhance campus habitats and encourage biodiversity and practices that limit campus habitats

THINK ABOUT IT

"A mind-boggling arsenal of fertilizers, pesticides, and herbicides, compounded largely since World War II, has been dumped on the breadbaskets of North America year after year."

—from *Seeds of Change*, edited by Herman J. Viola and Carolyn Margolis, Washington D.C.: Smithsonian Institution Press, p. 236

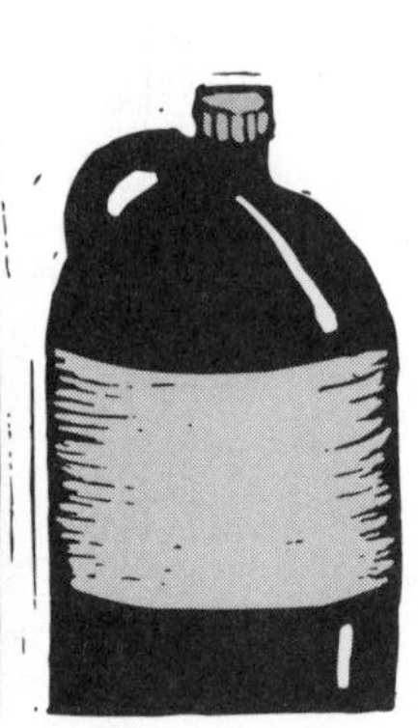

and threaten biodiversity. Select one member of your group to take notes, listing the pros and cons in two columns. For example, on the plus side, a flowering groundcover might prevent erosion, conserve water, and attract birds, butterflies, and insects. On the other hand, the playing field might require lots of water and chemical treatments and high maintenance that discourage wildlife.

C. When your group has completed its discussion, work together to write a one-page summary of your conclusions. Select someone from your group to present your summary to the rest of the class.

It's a Wrap

Discuss campus landscaping practices, pinpointing how habitats can be improved to encourage biodiversity. Then write a paragraph in your Journal telling how your summary addresses those topics.

Home

What could you do around your home to improve the surrounding landscape and encourage biodiversity? Write your ideas in your Journal.

Your teacher will give you a two-part activity sheet like the one below to use with this lesson.

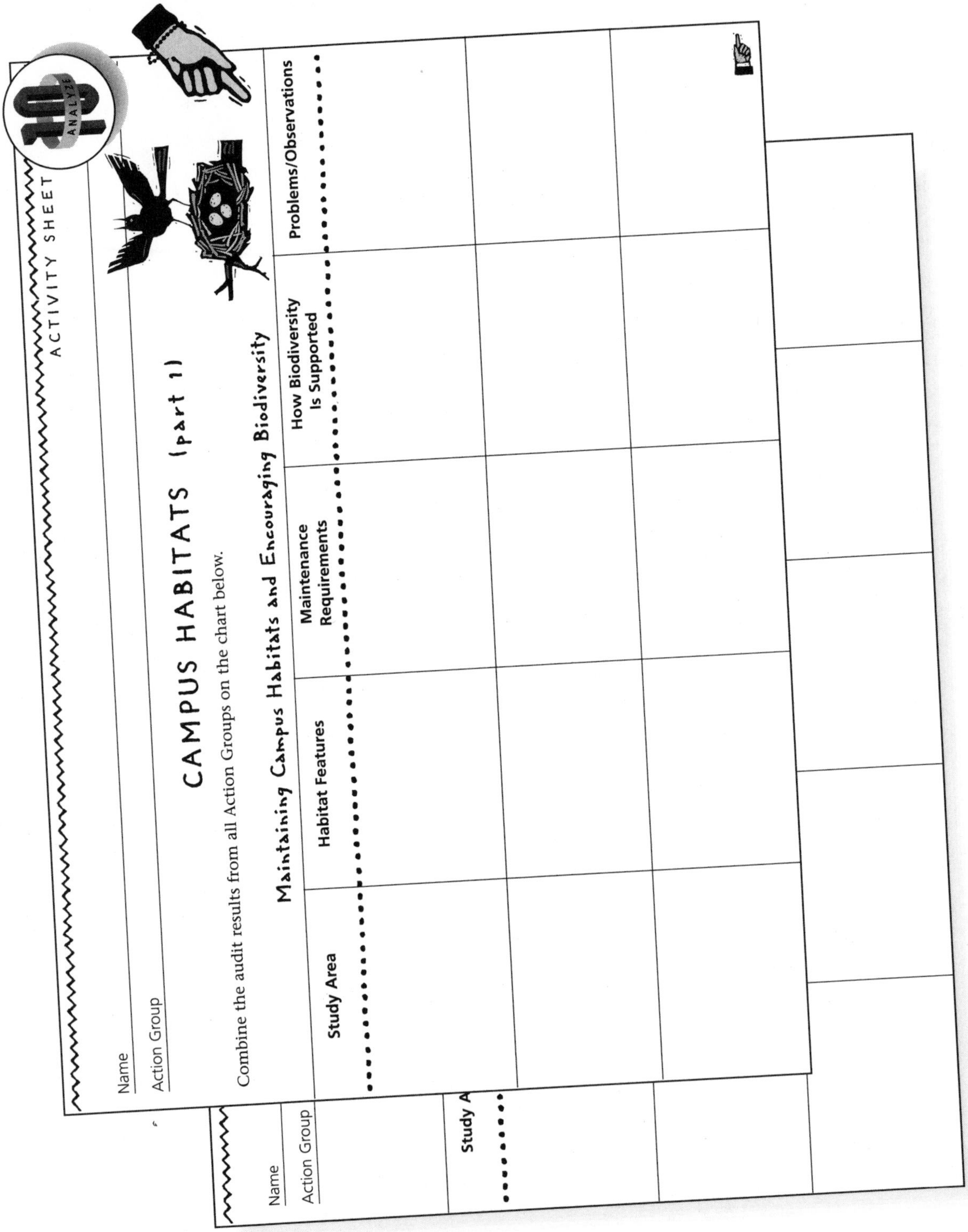

ACTIVITY SHEET

10 ANALYZE

Name

Action Group

CAMPUS HABITATS (part 1)

Combine the audit results from all Action Groups on the chart below.

Maintaining Campus Habitats and Encouraging Biodiversity

Study Area	Habitat Features	Maintenance Requirements	How Biodiversity Is Supported	Problems/Observations

Name

Action Group

Study A

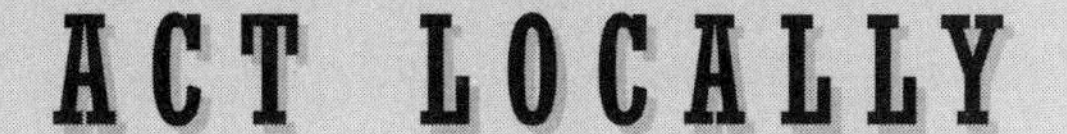

ACT LOCALLY

You've put a lot of work into finding out about campus habitats. Now share what you've learned with others in your school and community. With your class, plan a project that will increase awareness of habitats and encourage biodiversity, or use one of the following suggestions.

1. Organize a native plant sale at your school.
2. Organize a contest or raffle around the theme of preserving habitat and encouraging wildlife. Award conservation-related items, such as books and T-shirts, as prizes.
3. Take a tour of a local garden or nature center. Let them know about your audit and find out how they might be able to assist your efforts to enhance habitats on campus.

THINK ABOUT IT

"Waterwise gardening for wildlife is a complex subject, but those willing to get involved will be rewarded when their ordinary landscapes are transformed into delightful, easily maintained gardens full of mystery and magic."

—from *The Xeriscape Flower Gardener* by Jim Knopf, Boulder, CO: Johnson Books, 1991, p. 90

Consider Options

BRAINSTORM LANDSCAPING IDEAS

Find out what you can do to protect or enhance habitats found on the school campus. Investigate landscaping practices that will maintain or increase the biodiversity in those habitats.

Setting the Stage

Discuss these questions:

1. What landscaping practices can you suggest to increase biodiversity on your school campus?
2. What are the costs and benefits of your suggested landscaping practices?
3. How will protecting or enhancing campus habitats affect costs and benefits of landscaping practices?

Focus

A. Review the summaries from the previous activity. Look specifically at the problems associated with current landscaping practices. List the problems on the chalkboard. Have each Action Group tackle a different problem.

B. Meet with your Action Group and brainstorm solutions to each of the problems you have been assigned. Select a member of your group to take notes. Think about how landscaping practices can be changed to increase biodiversity and enhance habitats. What are the options? Are there better or more efficient ways to protect habitats and increase biodiversity? Use Activity Sheet 11 to write down your ideas for each problem.

C. After your group has finished brainstorming a list of options, go back and briefly evaluate the ideas. Cross out those that are clearly unworkable or impractical. Then complete Activity Sheet 11. Find out names of

THINK ABOUT IT

"Providing hedgerows, woodlots, streamside habitat, and shade trees in an agricultural landscape can provide cover and nesting areas for birds."

—from The Smithsonian Migratory Bird Center Fact Sheet No. 2, Washington, D.C.

books, people, landscaping and garden companies and organizations that can aid your investigation. Divide up the responsibility for this investigation. You may choose to work individually or with a partner.

As you conduct this research, ask yourself the following questions for each landscaping idea:

1. What current landscaping practice prompted the need for a change?
2. What are benefits of this plan in terms of increasing biodiversity and maintaining habitats?
3. Are any pieces of equipment and/or materials needed? If so, how will we get them?
4. How much time is needed to put the plan into action?
5. What is the estimated cost of the plan (including labor) and how can the items be paid for? Can they be donated or loaned?
6. Who is responsible for making the plan happen, including maintenance and repair?

It's a Wrap

You have been investigating landscaping practices for your study area. If you could make just one change at the site, what would it be? What change would have the biggest effect on increasing biodiversity or improving the habitat? Record your ideas in your Journal.

Home

Identify three landscaping practices at or near your home that help to increase biodiversity. Identify three landscaping practices that could help to protect the habitat at or near your home.

Your teacher will give you an activity sheet like the one below to use with this lesson.

ACTIVITY SHEET

CONSIDER OPTIONS

Name

Action Group

LANDSCAPING OPTIONS

Use the following chart to help you organize your ideas while brainstorming landscaping options.

Problem:

	Options	Research
Landscaping Practices that will Increase Biodiversity		Who will research? Information Sources
Landscaping Practices that will Preserve or Restore Habitat		Who will research? Information Sources

WEIGH THE COSTS AND BENEFITS

You have gathered information about landscaping practices that will enhance habitat and increase biodiversity. Now you will work with your Action Group to evaluate the costs and benefits of the options you have investigated.

Setting the Stage

Discuss these questions:

1. Can you measure or put a value on nonmonetary costs and benefits? Explain your answer.
2. Why is it important to consider both long- and short-term effects before choosing a landscaping plan?

Focus

Report back to your Action Group on the landscaping options you have explored. As a group, combine your findings and do a cost-benefit analysis for each option. Select a member of your group to take notes. While doing your analysis, keep in mind that there are often hidden costs or benefits. The following questions can help you analyze costs and benefits:

1. Who will be affected by the change? How?
2. If the option calls for changing people's habits, how will you get them to cooperate? Is this a cost or a benefit?
3. What are the nonmonetary benefits of this option?
4. What are the nonmonetary costs of this option?
5. Are there any long-term costs or benefits?

To help you evaluate the options for solving each problem, complete Activity Sheet 12 as a group.

THINK ABOUT IT

"Every day in America, 2750 acres of land are paved. When that happens, birds, animals and insects lose their habitats."

—Eco Fact from *Eco Warrior*, Vol. 1, No. 1, St. Paul, MN: Eco Education, April 1994, p. 7

It's a Wrap

With the class, discuss the importance of assessing nonmonetary costs and benefits and summarize how your group has taken them into account in your analysis of the landscaping options. Then discuss the importance of looking at both the long- and the short-term effects of the landscaping options you recommend.

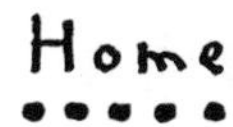

Would any of the alternative landscaping ideas that you learned about be appropriate for your home? Write a description of how you might use one of these ideas at your home.

Your teacher will give you an activity sheet like the one below to use with this lesson.

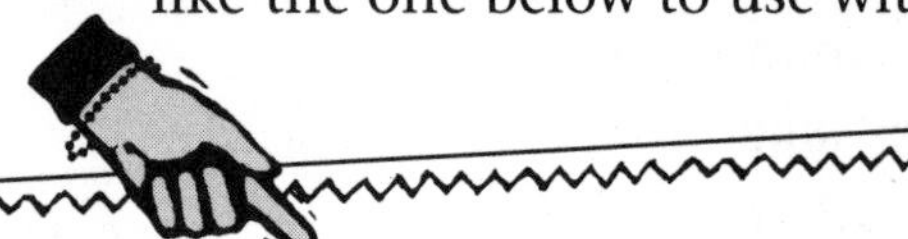

ACTIVITY SHEET

CONSIDER OPTIONS 12

Name

Action Group

ASSESS COSTS AND BENEFITS

Use the following chart to evaluate the costs and benefits of each landscaping problem and the options for solving it.

Problem:

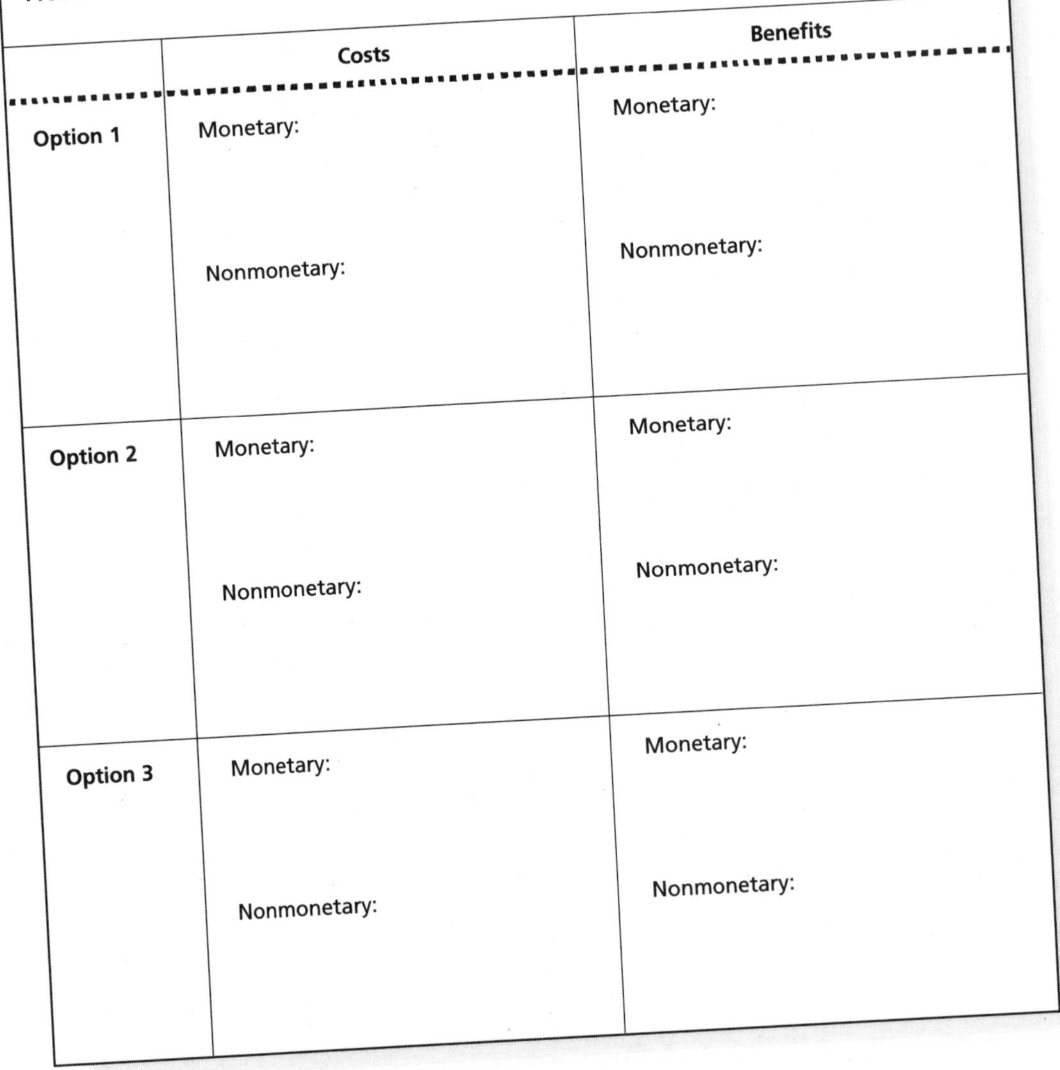

	Costs	Benefits
Option 1	Monetary: Nonmonetary:	Monetary: Nonmonetary:
Option 2	Monetary: Nonmonetary:	Monetary: Nonmonetary:
Option 3	Monetary: Nonmonetary:	Monetary: Nonmonetary:

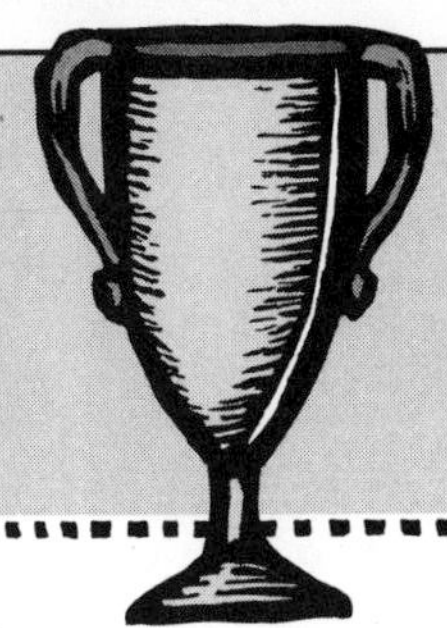

MAKE RECOMMENDATIONS

During this activity, your Action Group will give final consideration to all the landscaping options you've been exploring. After weighing the costs and benefits of each, you'll select the best ones and develop a finished proposal for presenting your recommendations to your class.

> **THINK ABOUT IT**
>
> "...95% of our global nutritional requirements are derived from a mere 30 kinds of plants and three-quarters of our diet is based upon only eight crops—a far cry from the 80,000 plants the world offers as potential edible species."
>
> —from *GAIA: An Atlas of Planet Management*, edited by Dr. Norman Myers, Anchor Books/Doubleday, 1984, p. 145

Setting the Stage

Discuss these questions:

1. How can you decide the best landscaping strategies to implement?
2. Are the lowest-cost options always the best choices? Why or why not?

Focus

A. Meet with your Action Group and review the cost-benefit analyses that you completed for each problem assigned to your group. Which options do you consider to be the best solutions to each problem?

B. Prepare a convincing presentation of your ideas to give to the rest of your class. Begin by completing the Landscaping Proposal on Activity Sheet 13 to detail your proposal. You may want to enhance your presentation by adding diagrams, illustrations, tables, charts, graphs, and other graphic materials to demonstrate the advantages of your proposal.

It's a Wrap

Share with the class how your Action Group evaluated options and considered costs and benefits as options were assessed. Did every group use the same criteria? After the

discussion, write a summary in your Journal of your personal responses to the questions posed in Setting the Stage.

Home

Think of ways that you can document or record a part of the natural world around your home (photographs, pressed flowers, sketches). Keep this record in your Journal.

Your teacher will give you an activity sheet like the one below to use with this lesson.

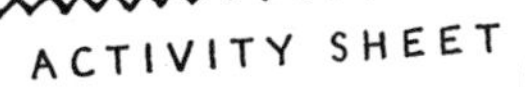

Name

Action Group

LANDSCAPING PROPOSAL

Use the space below to provide specific data about the proposal your group is making to enhance habitats and increase biodiversity on campus. You will want to include diagrams, graphs, charts, and other graphic organizers to pinpoint the benefits of your proposal.

Problem:

Solution:

Implementation of Proposal

Action Required:

Cost:

Long-term Maintenance (costs and labor):

Type of Habitat

Current Landscaping:

Proposed Change:

Benefit:

Effect on Biodiversity:

Other Benefits:

ACT LOCALLY

You have now had the opportunity to explore a wide range of landscaping ideas designed to enhance habitats and increase biodiversity. Share some of your ideas with your schoolmates and members of your community by carrying out a project such as one of the following.

1. Create a one- or two-page list of environmentally friendly landscaping and garden resources—the address of an heirloom seed company, a list of plants that attract butterflies and birds, a pamphlet about how to restore a stream habitat—and include it in the school newspaper or distribute it as a flyer to students.
2. Participate in an organized community group activity aimed at protecting or enhancing the environment, such as a hike, fund-raiser, or clean-up activity.
3. Organize a "clean-up the campus" day at your school.

THINK ABOUT IT

"A pesticide-free, naturally-balanced garden, with a variety of low-water-use, flowering plants—especially natives—can be a haven for native birds, beneficial insects and other creatures."

—from "What Is Sustainable Landscaping?" by Rick Fisher, Owen Dell and Lili Singer in *The Southern California Gardener*, Volume 2, Number 6, July–August 1993, p. 3

Take Action

CHOOSE LANDSCAPING MEASURES

Your Action Group will present its ideas about landscaping practices that enhance habitats and increase biodiversity so that the class can decide which measures to present to the school committee.

Setting the Stage

Discuss these questions:

1. What factors need to be considered when deciding on which landscaping practices to recommend?
2. What will help make a landscaping recommendation successful?

Focus

Each Action Group is going to present its landscaping ideas to the class. Use Activity Sheet 14 to make notes and rate each group's ideas on a scale of 1 to 3. Also jot down any questions you want to discuss further as you decide which ideas are the best. Once all the presentations have been made and evaluated, you and your classmates will discuss the proposals and reach a consensus on which measures to propose to the school committee.

THINK ABOUT IT

"The practiced eye can observe the native plant in its nearby natural surroundings to learn the conditions that suit it best."

—from *Gardening with Native Plants of the Pacific Northwest* by Arthur R. Kruckeberg, Seattle: University of Washington Press, 1982, p. 17

It's a Wrap

Review the information presented, along with your impressions of and opinions about the measures you will propose. Write a paragraph or draw a cartoon illustrating how your landscaping practices will successfully enhance campus habitats and increase biodiversity.

Home

Read a magazine or newspaper article about landscaping or garden practices. Write a summary of it in your Journal.

Your teacher will give you an activity sheet like the one below to use with this lesson.

ACTIVITY SHEET

14 TAKE ACTION

Name

RATING SHEET

Fill in the following rating sheet for each presentation.

Group

Plan

Costs

Expensive • • • Inexpensive

Environmental Benefits

Low • • • High

Impact on Habitat and Biodiversity

Low • • • High

Difficulty of Implementing

Low • • • High

Cooperation Incentives

Low • • • High

Effectiveness of Presentation

Low • • • High

Additional Factors to Consider

Priority

Low • • • High

PREPARE AND PRESENT YOUR PROPOSAL

Now that you have explored landscaping options and decided on which plans your class will recommend for the school, use your powers of persuasion to draft a proposal and to present it to your school committee.

Setting the Stage

Discuss these questions:

1. What factors had the most serious impact on habitat and biodiversity of the site you audited?
2. How will the landscaping ideas you are proposing provide both short- and long-term solutions?
3. What were the most important reasons for choosing these measures?

Focus

Think about these questions as you plan your presentation:

1. What will be the most effective plan for organizing the presentation? Should you begin with the problem, provide the solution, and then outline the costs and savings? Would another order be more persuasive?
2. What is the most important idea you want to emphasize? The importance of preserving habitats? The importance of increasing biodiversity? The ease and low cost of implementing a particular idea?
3. How can you use charts, graphs, tables, and diagrams to illustrate and promote your ideas?
4. What tone will be the most persuasive?

Keep these ideas in mind as you and your classmates work together to create an outline. Use the outline on page 63 as a guide.

THINK ABOUT IT

"In general, the greater the diversity of the landscape, the greater the variety of wildlife that will be interested in the landscape."

—from The *Xeriscape Flower Gardener* by Jim Knopf, Boulder, CO: Johnson Books, 1991, p. 88

I. Title
II. Introduction
III. Recommendation
Include information about cost, benefits, step-by-step implementation, opportunity for participation, need for cooperation, maintenance.

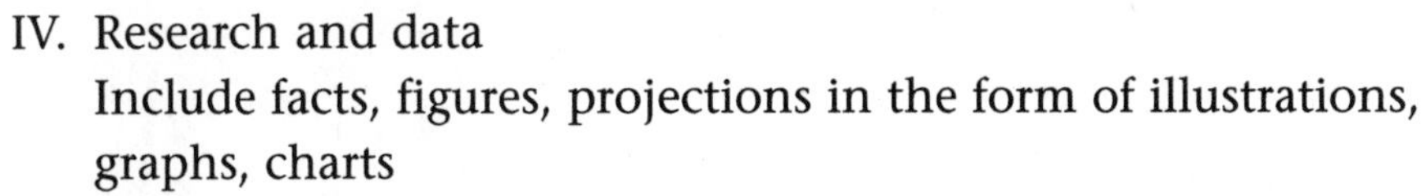

IV. Research and data
Include facts, figures, projections in the form of illustrations, graphs, charts
V. Description of habitat-related activities already underway.

With your classmates, decide what tasks need to be done and in what order. Then divide up responsibility and prepare the proposal. Use Activity Sheet 15 to keep track of progress.

It's a Wrap

When all the elements of the proposal are complete, carefully review each part and discuss and make any final changes. Be sure that you have included sufficient details to support your main points. Then present your proposal to the school committee.

Home

Write a letter about habitat and biodiversity issues to a city official, state or congressional representative, or even to the President. Describe what you like about his or her preservation or enhancement efforts, or make specific suggestions about how habitat management policies can be improved. Put a copy of your letter in your Journal.

Your teacher will give you a two-part activity sheet like the one below to use with this lesson.

ACTIVITY SHEET

Name

PROPOSAL CHECKLIST (part 1)

Use this checklist to plan and monitor tasks that may need to be done in order to complete your proposal. Make a note of who is responsible for completing each task, when each task should be completed, materials needed, and so on. Add to the list as needed.

TASKS	NOTES
1. TITLE ☐ Cover illustration ☐ Proposal statement	
2. WRITE THE INTRODUCTORY PARAGRAPH. ☐ Explain the project. ☐ Briefly describe audit findings.	
3. WRITE RECOMMENDATIONS. ☐ Outline each plan. ☐ Highlight the benefits. ☐ Specify the costs. ☐ Suggest a step-by-step plan for implementation. ☐ Include ideas for motivating student body, increasing awareness, and encouraging participation. ☐ Outline long-range maintenance requirements, costs, planning. ☐ Pinpoint projected savings.	

Continue your recommendations on next page.

TRACK RESPONSE TO PROPOSAL

You have recommended to your school committee landscaping ideas that enhance habitats and increase biodiversity, and you have outlined a plan for implementing and maintaining them. Now put your efforts into increasing awareness among the school population and working toward implementing your proposals.

Setting the Stage

Discuss these questions:

1. How can you find out what effect your landscaping ideas are having?
2. How can you assess the level of awareness and participation in enhancing habitats and increasing biodiversity?

Focus

Discuss the landscaping proposals that you developed and presented to the committee. How can other students and staff in your school be motivated to continue to support habitat enhancement? How can student participation be increased? Use Activity Sheet 16 to summarize the results of your proposals and to keep track of progress over time.

It's a Wrap

With your classmates, discuss the success of your landscaping plans. What are the most surprising benefits? What would make the plans more effective? In your Journal, write three ideas for increasing awareness of habitat and biodiversity issues.

THINK ABOUT IT

"If diversity is to be saved, it may well be by the direct individual actions of visionary botanists and biologists and committed back-yard gardeners creating a green necklace of living gardens in newly grown centers of diversity around the world."

—from *Seeds of Change 1994 Catalog*, Kenny Ausubel, ed., p. 55

Home

What can you do? Besides all of the activities that you and your classmates have planned, think of three ideas for action that promote the preservation of habitat and biodiversity, either at home or in your community. Record your ideas in your Journal.

Your teacher will give you a two-part activity sheet like the one below to use with this lesson.

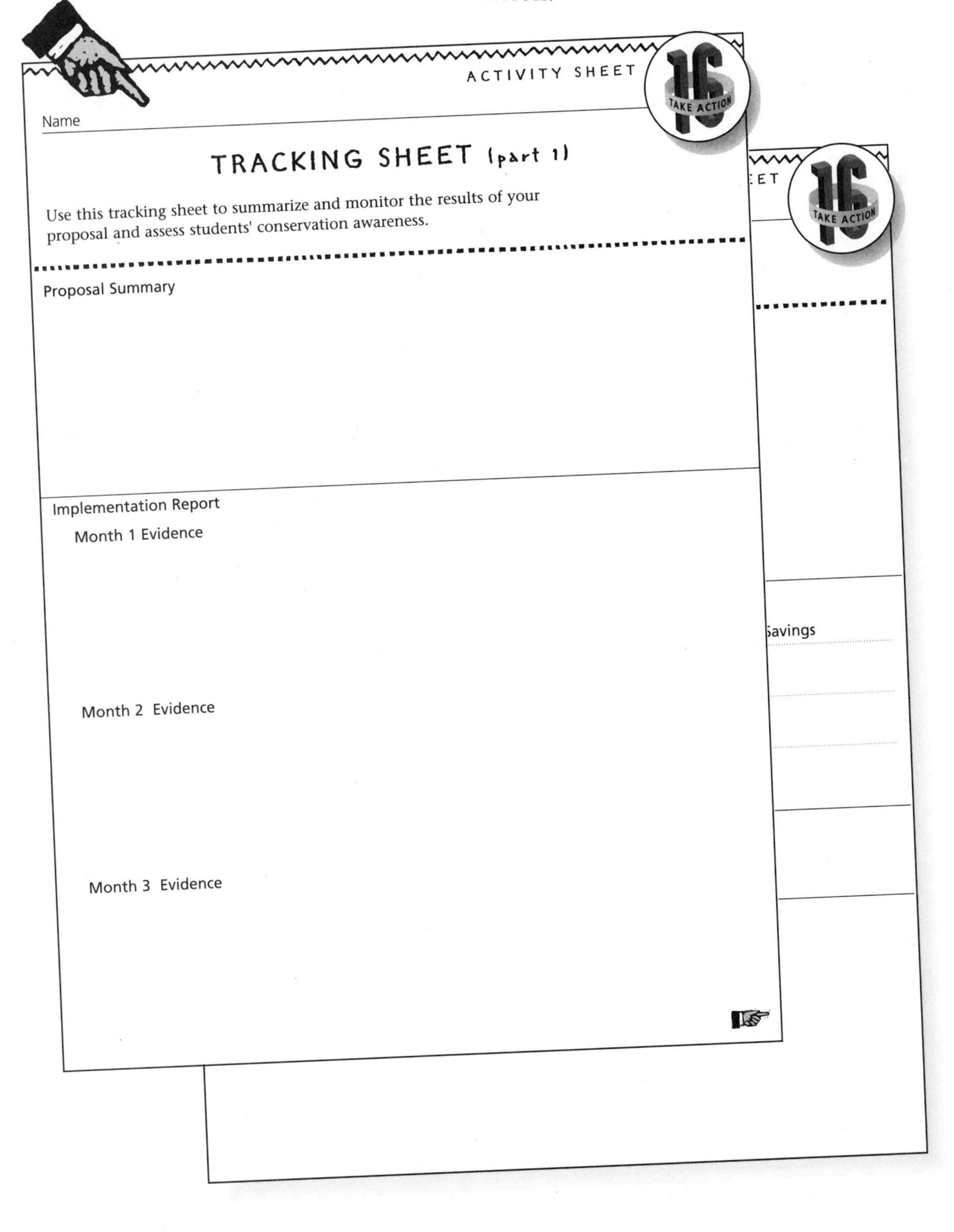
ACTIVITY SHEET

16 TAKE ACTION

Name

TRACKING SHEET (part 1)

Use this tracking sheet to summarize and monitor the results of your proposal and assess students' conservation awareness.

Proposal Summary

Implementation Report

Month 1 Evidence

Month 2 Evidence

Month 3 Evidence

Issues and Information

Section A
BIODIVERSITY

Biodiversity is the term used to describe the incredible variety of life on earth—the tremendous array of plants, animals, and ecosystems. It is almost impossible to imagine earth without this rich abundance and variety of life, yet biodiversity is a natural resource that is seriously threatened today. Biodiversity is as much in need of protection as our air, land, and water.

Biodiversity exists at three different levels: ecosystem diversity, species diversity, and genetic diversity. Learning about these different levels will help you understand the full importance of biodiversity.

Ecosystem diversity An ecosystem is a community of living organisms in a particular environment and the nonliving things with which it interacts. A desert, for instance, is an ecosystem that includes organisms such as cacti, lizards, and birds and nonliving parts such as sandy soil, rocks, and sunlight. Ecosystem diversity is used to refer to the various large categories of ecosystems called biomes, such as a desert or rain forest, as well as smaller ecosystems, such as a riverbank or the north side of a mountain. The organisms in an ecosystem depend on each other and on the nonliving parts for survival. (See Section B for more information on ecosystems and biomes.)

Species diversity Species diversity is often what is meant when the term biodiversity is used. Species diversity is the remarkable variety of species of living things—plants, animals, fungi, and microorganisms. It is not known how many different species there are on earth. Over 1.4 million have been identified, and millions have yet to be determined. In the 1980s scientists estimated there were about 5 million species in total. But as they have done more studies, especially in tropical forests where species diversity is enormous, their estimates have gone up and up—to over 30 million. In fact, some research suggests there may be 30 million species of insects alone.

Genetic diversity Each individual organism has thousands of genes that determine its characteristics—its color, height, weight, shape, resistance to disease, and so forth. A common group of genes, called the gene pool, exists for each species. Individual members of a species

develop with different genes drawn from the gene pool, which results in genetic diversity. Because of this genetic diversity, organisms can evolve and adapt to changes in their environment, including developing the ability to survive diseases.

Wild plants and animals have more varied characteristics,—that is, more genetic diversity—than cultivated ones. Individual plants of a cultivated plant crop, for example, all have the same genes, and none may have the characteristic to fight a particular disease. If a disease strikes the crop, as occurred in the corn blight in the U.S. in 1970, the entire crop may be lost. Many of the types of tomatoes we eat today would have been lost except for the introduction into their breeding of the genes of a wild Peruvian tomato resistant to disease. The abundant genetic diversity found in wild organisms is the building block for the continuing evolution of life on earth.

Why Is Biodiversity Important?

Many people would say that the importance of biodiversity is obvious. We experience the value of biodiversity constantly in our enjoyment of nature—in walking in the park, taking trips to the zoo or a wild area, working in our gardens, playing with our pets, reading books and watching TV shows about wondrous creatures in foreign lands. We marvel at nature's diversity. Some believe that biodiversity should be protected just because it is so wonderful. Some say biodiversity is important for other philosophical or spiritual reasons—for a reverence for life and a moral obligation not to destroy what has been created. But there are many other reasons why biodiversity is important.

Think in terms of the three kinds of biodiversity, for instance. Loss in any of these types of biodiversity disrupts the balance of life. If an ecosystem is destroyed, all the organisms adapted to that ecosystem are likely to be destroyed as well. If a species is lost, all the other species whose lives depend on interactions with it may be lost. If it is what scientists call a "keystone" species, the existence of a whole ecosystem may depend on it. If a gene pool is lost or reduced, the genes that make it possible for species to survive through adaptations to changing environments are lost. The loss of genetic diversity, in fact, is considered by many people today to be the greatest threat to the long-range health of our planet.

Biodiversity is also important for the countless direct benefits it provides to humans. The great variety of earth's plants give us the air we breathe; animals and plants give us the food we eat; and a whole array of organisms and microorganisms cleanse the water we drink, regulate floods, recycle waste, and control pests.

Biodiversity also gives us economic and health benefits. Agriculture depends on the genetic diversity of wild plants to improve cultivated crops. Industries, such as wood products and rubber, depend on raw materials from wild plants. Medicine is particularly dependent on biodiversity. Over 40 percent of prescription drugs in the U.S. have been derived from wild species, and new medical treatments from such sources are constantly being discovered.

Many organisms that were once thought to be "useless"—like the penicillium mold or the tropical bat that pollinates precious Asian fruits—have proven to be very valuable. And that is the further tragedy of today's rapid loss of biodiversity—we are losing species before we have any idea what their importance might be.

Extinction and the Loss of Biodiversity

Extinction is the natural process of species disappearing from the earth—organisms become extinct and new organisms evolve. Before humans appeared on earth, major extinctions were caused by natural environmental changes and occurred over hundreds of years. Today, people's activities—mainly the destruction of habitats—are causing the extinction of species at a rate some researchers suggest is about 400 times the natural rate. This rapid rate of extinction means an alarming loss of biodiversity; nature cannot evolve new species quickly enough to replace those that are being destroyed.

The rate of species extinction has risen steeply from about 400 per year in 1980 to over 10,000 per year in 1990. Some scientists estimate that we are currently losing as many as 17,500 species each year; others estimate that by the year 2000, if human habitat destruction continues as its present rate, the loss of species could be as high as 50,000 each year—or about 130 species every day.

Some researchers estimate that we could lose more than 25 percent of all species on earth within the next few decades. This massive extinction represents a greater biological loss than any in geologic history, including the disappearance of the dinosaurs and other forms of life 65 million years ago. (See section C for further information on the threats to biodiversity and causes of extinction.)

Section B

BIOMES, BIOREGIONS, AND HABITATS

In earlier times, people knew their own regions intimately. They knew when plants flowered or seeds matured, when fruits ripened, where birds nested and where fish returned to spawn. They depended on this knowledge of the land, plants, and animals around them to provide all their needs. Some people today are trying to regain some of this closer relationship to their environment by living more simply on the land, raising their own food, or by buying only foods that are locally grown, such as those available at a farmer's market. But generally we are much less well acquainted with our own regions today. What plants and animals live in your region? Which of these were there before humans arrived? Which have been introduced? What is the annual rainfall? What makes up the soil? When does the first flower bloom in spring?

Biomes

One way to start the study of the region you live in is by identifying which region you are in according to biologists' classifications of the different regions on earth. The land-based regions on earth are classified into large communities called biomes. Each biome is distinguished by its climate (temperature and rainfall patterns) and its communities of plants and animals. Biologists identify between about six and twelve biomes, depending on the level of detail they are using. Nine biomes typically identified are

- tundra
- taiga
- temperate coniferous forest
- temperate deciduous forest
- chaparral
- desert
- grassland
- savanna
- tropical rain forest

Biomes include areas in different regions of the world. There is tundra, for example, on flat land in the Arctic as well as high on the tops of mountains in many different countries. Each biome has similar types of plants and animals, but individual species vary from area to area.

Biomes and Biodiversity

The different climates and geographic characteristics of the various ecosystems and biomes in a sense cause biodiversity. When plants and animals evolve and adapt to the characteristics of their particular regions, they become different from species in other regions, and thus biodiversity is increased. Many organisms become so specialized to their regions that they cannot survive anywhere else.

The regions with the greatest biodiversity are the tropical rain forests, wetland environments, and the coral reefs in the ocean. Biologists estimate that perhaps two-thirds or more of all species on earth live in tropical rain forests. Twenty-five acres of tropical forest were found to have as many tree species as there are in all of North America; one tropical tree was found to have 43 different kinds of ants; 19 trees to have 12,000 types of beetles; and one river to have more fish species than all the rivers in the U.S. It is probably the relative warmth and abundance of water in tropical forests, wetlands, and coral reef areas that makes them able to support a greater variety of life forms than other regions. Because these delicate environments teem with life, damage to them causes particularly great losses in biodiversity.

The biodiversity of species is distributed unevenly over the globe. The biomes closest to the equator—the rain forests—have the greatest species diversity. The biomes farthest away—the ice and tundra of the Arctic and Antarctic—have the least species diversity. Although scientists do not fully understand the reasons for this uneven distribution of species, the year-round warmth and moisture in the tropical areas may explain it. Without the cold of winter to contend with, organisms can grow and reproduce in the tropics year-round. Insects, for example, can complete their life cycles in a very short time.

Bioregions and Habitats

Once you have identified your biome, to further study your region you will want to look at the special characteristics unique to your area and the homes of the living organisms around you. Within any biome are

numerous bioregions—areas with a unique set of plants, animals, weather conditions, soil conditions, and geographic features such as hills, mountains, lakes, wetlands, or valleys. Animals and plants that have evolved naturally in a particular bioregion are called native plants or animals.

Within any bioregion are more specialized areas that are homes for each organism. These homes are called habitats. The characteristics of a habitat include such features as special soil conditions, light conditions, temperatures, quality and availability of air or water, and the presence of other organisms. The habitat for a bird would be where it has the food, water, shelter, and nesting site it needs. The habitat for a particular shrub might be in the shade where it is very cool and moist—perhaps on the north side but not the south side of a building. A butterfly's habitat might require the presence of a specific plant for its nectar. The habitat for a worm would be underground in certain types of soil.

Habitats for some plants or animals are very specialized; other organisms can live in a variety of habitats. Many organisms—particularly plants—provide the habitat for other organisms. An oak tree often provides the habitat for many different organisms—lichens, mosses, birds, many types of insects, spiders, lizards, rodents; a green lawn might provide the habitat for fewer organisms—a few types of insects, spiders, worms. You will learn a great deal about the different habitats in your area by undertaking the adventure of closely observing and studying the patterns of life in each one.

Section C
THREATS TO BIODIVERSITY

Species have always—and will always—die out. They become extinct because of competition with other species and not being able to adapt to environmental changes. Natural events such as shifts in climate or natural disasters (such as major floods or fires) can cause species to be lost. The natural process of extinction usually occurs over many years.

Effects of Civilization on Biodiversity

As the human population has expanded and required more food and other goods, the rate of species extinction has grown well beyond the natural rate. The primary cause of this rapid loss of biodiversity is the human destruction of habitats. We destroy habitats when we cut down forests for fuel or timber or to create farm or ranch land. We destroy habitats by damming waterways; by draining wetlands; by building roads and cities; and by polluting the air, land, and water. Habitats are being destroyed or damaged in every part of the earth, including the Antarctic and the Arctic. We destroy habitats with the intention of improving or enriching civilization—for products, for food, for homes—but instead we are destroying the very biodiversity that ensures the future of healthy life on earth. (See section A for further information biodiversity and extinction.)

Overexploitation—excessive harvesting or hunting of particular species—is another human activity that threatens biodiversity. The survival of whales has been threatened because of overharvesting for their oil, for example, just as elephants have been overharvested for their ivory tusks, otters for their fur, and various cacti and tropical birds for their beauty. Overharvesting of the trees in a forest causes the destruction of the entire forest habitat.

Another human threat to biodiversity is the introduction of non-native species of plants or animals to an environment—sometimes on purpose and other times by accident, such as by carrying seeds stuck to clothing or insects aboard cargo ships. The nonnative species may have no enemies in the new environment, and the native species have no defenses against the nonnatives. Thus, the nonnative species may

spread quickly, competing with and destroying native species. For example, a third of the native bird species in Hawaii have become extinct due to nonnative snakes, pigs, and other animals brought in on ships from other countries. Similarly, the Oriental kudzu vine, introduced into the southeastern U.S., has become a serious pest, threatening the survival of many other plants.

The Special Case of Tropical Forests

Because tropical forests are home to such a tremendous variety of species—possibly over 60 percent of all species on earth—the destruction of habitat in tropical forests is the cause of the greatest loss of biodiversity today. Tropical rain forests are being destroyed primarily for fuel; for range land; for land for agriculture; and for the timber to make furniture, paper, and other goods. At least 40 percent of the tropical forests on earth have already been destroyed, and we are destroying something like another 20 hectares (49 acres) every minute. The loss of biodiversity due to human destruction of habitat in the tropical forests is staggering.

A Lesson From the Past

We often think of ancient civilizations as less exploiting of the environment than our civilization, but archeological research shows that ancient people, too, caused increased species extinction by clear-cutting forests, overharvesting plants and animals, and destroying habitats. We may have a particular lesson to learn from these findings, in fact, for in some cases, the loss of habitat and biodiversity caused by some ancient civilizations may have brought about their own extinction.

One case is that of the extraordinary civilization of the early Maya people in Central America. No one is certain why their culture collapsed around 1600 after thriving for thousands of years, but recent studies have shown that over 80 percent of the forests where they lived had been destroyed. Archaeologists speculate that the loss of the forests may have caused erosion of the soil and thus severely damaged the Mayas' ability to grow corn and other crops important to their survival. Another case is that of the ancient Anasazi people in the southwestern United States. Their overhunting of tigers, mammoths, and bears and overharvesting of vast forest resources may have similarly forced them to leave the sites of their early impressive civilization.

Section D

CONSERVING BIODIVERSITY

Scientists are pointing out that conservation of biodiversity needs to be part of how we plan, use, and enhance our natural resources everywhere. People are taking steps to conserve biodiversity by protecting wild habitats, establishing protection laws, and enriching biodiversity in their local areas with parks, gardens, and landscapes. They are also trying new ways of gardening, landscaping, using land, and harvesting wildlife that do as little damage to the natural ecosystems as possible. These new methods are called "sustainable" because they allow the populations and habitats to be sustained for the future.

Protect Habitat

One of the most important ways to conserve biodiversity is to prevent further loss by protecting wild habitats. Many environmental organizations and governments around the world are working to safeguard natural areas. So far, however, only about three percent of land on earth is protected. And some biomes have much more protected land than others. Notably, there is very little protected land in the rain forest and grassland biomes. Protecting wild habitats is the best way to preserve species, genetic, and ecosystem diversity.

Establish Protection Laws

The Endangered Species Act in the U.S. is a good example of a law established to protect biodiversity. Species whose survival is threatened are protected under this law because, as the act says, they are of "aesthetic, ecological, educational, historical, recreational, and scientific value to the Nation and its people." International laws, based on treaties and conventions, also protect wildlife. Many people feel

strongly about protecting some of the endangered species such as the giant panda, the mountain gorilla, and the California condor, but many of the less sensational, less charming endangered or threatened organisms are equally important to human and environmental survival.

Practice Sustainable Gardening and Landscaping

People can enhance the biodiversity of their own communities by planting and caring for gardens and landscapes, especially those that imitate the local bioregion. For example, an area of native plants, maintained without pesticides, will become a habitat for many birds and other animals of the region. Similarly, a landscape of plants that mimic the habits and needs of natives—such as drought-tolerant plants in an area with little rainfall—will have the least damaging impact on local resources and provide habitat for other organisms. Gardening not only enriches our environment, it also helps us to understand and appreciate the workings of nature. Issues and Information sections G and H provide more information about practicing sustainable gardening and landscaping.

Practice Sustainable Harvesting

New sustainable methods of harvesting wildlife are being tried which do not threaten the survival of a species or its ecosystem. Many of these experimental methods do not succeed because of the difficulty of having a thorough knowledge of all the interactions of an intricate ecosystem. But some new methods are succeeding, and it is an important effort to find alternatives to overharvesting. For example, domesticated blue fox are being raised on ranches rather than killing the wild fox for their fur. For another example, selective methods of hunting—taking only a sustainable harvest—have maintained a thriving population of North American deer.

Take Action at the Local Level: What YOU Can Do

Start a Project

- Visit a nearby arboretum or botanical garden. Then turn the school campus into an arboretum or botanical garden with signs identifying the variety of trees, shrubs, or other plants. Identify which species are native.
- Use local gardens and parks as the focal point for celebrations and meetings.
- Help to beautify an old cemetery.
- Reclaim a vacant lot and create a community garden where plots can be used on a seasonal or yearly basis.
- Identify the habitats of birds and put up and maintain bird feeders or birdbaths in the areas where they perch and feed. Learn the names of the birds that come to feed or bathe.

Work with Others

- Get involved with wildlife or gardening organizations.
- Adopt a nearby park and help the park administrators in their beautification efforts, lending a wildlife habitat perspective.
- Adopt a stream and work with city officials to beautify or maintain it or to educate people about how to keep it clean.
- Participate in wildlife appreciation activities such as birding, photography, and whale watching.
- Volunteer for a wildlife rehabilitation organization or an animal shelter.
- Visit and support local and national public lands such as National Wildlife Refuges, Forests, and Parks.

Educate Yourself and Others

- Write or talk to elected officials about your interest in biodiversity, habitat protection, and natural resource conservation.
- Find out about local habitat-related issues. Express your concern about such issues by writing elected officials or the newspaper.
- Learn more about endangered species by visiting aquariums, botanical gardens, and zoos.

- Educate yourself about products that come from endangered animals and plants, such as coral, furs, exotic shells, cacti, orchids, reptile skins, ivory, tropical birds, and things made of mahogany. Avoid buying those products unless you know they are from a responsible, ecologically safe source.
- Find out about fish and wildlife governmental agencies or programs that protect endangered or threatened species or habitats.
- Teach someone else about the importance of genetic diversity, endangered species, and the preservation of habitats.

Be a Plant Planter

- Work with the local municipality to organize tree plantings around town. Planting deciduous trees on the southern side of buildings and evergreens on the northern side helps to moderate temperatures in both summer and winter.
- Plant trees, shrubs, or flowers that will attract birds, butterflies, and other animals.
- Design and plant a special garden for small children, elderly people, or people with disabilities. For example, plants that are scented or have an interesting texture could be planted for blind people to enjoy.
- Plant a garden to preserve and demonstrate genetic diversity by using traditional varieties of flowers, fruits, and vegetables and maintaining a seed storage system.
- Plant colorful, low-water maintenance flowering plants to help beautify traffic islands and other public spaces such as community centers, hospitals, and libraries.
- Plant native plants, especially native wildflowers. These plants require little maintenance and water.
- Instead of fences, plant rows of shrubs or trees.

Be Wild!

- Work with others to leave some areas—large or small—wild and uncultivated as habitat for insects, reptiles, birds, and other native species.
- Join with others to preserve an important natural area such as a wetland, a grove of ancient trees, or a habitat for an endangered species.

Section E
PLANTS

To choose plants that are right for your area and for your purpose, you will want to consult books, magazines, local gardening organizations or agricultural extension offices, nurseries, gardening friends, or other experts. The U.S. Department of Agriculture and other organizations divide areas of the country into different hardiness zones or climate zones.

Reference books and nurseries categorize plants by these zones as well as by how much sun or shade and how much water they need. The plants for your garden need to be ones that are hardy in your climate and in your chosen spot.

There will be many plants to choose from for your area. A good way to sort through the selection is to think of what you want in terms of the plants' sizes, shapes, and growth habits. Other considerations for your plant selections might include some special qualities you want in your plants. Here are some examples of qualities to consider:

- Native plants: You might want native plants not only for their beauty but also because they are adapted to your area, because of their attractions for wildlife, and because they tend to be low-maintenance.
- Plants for color at different times of year: Plants may be chosen for their colors including the color of their flowers, their fruits and berries, their year-round leaves, their leaves in autumn, or their bark.
- Plants that produce edible fruits, leaves, roots, and other parts: Popular food plants include tomatoes, beans, lettuce, radishes, potatoes, and squashes. Fruit trees such as plum, cherry, and apple thrive in some areas as well.
- Ground covers and lawn substitutes: Grass lawns are well-suited for areas that are walked and played on frequently. Some types of grass are more disease or drought-tolerant than others, but all lawns require a good deal of water and maintenance. There are many ground covers other than grass, some of them producing flowers,

some growing as flat mats, others as knee-high clusters of plants, and many requiring less water and care.

- Plants that produce special fragrances: Many plants are noted for their fragrances—some sweet, some spicy, some resembling other odors such as coffee or lemons. Plants generally are most fragrant in sunny, humid weather. Fragrant plants include lavender, sweet pea, daphne, honeysuckle, gardenia, lilac, mock orange, jasmine, peony, and, of course, roses.
- Plants that attract wildlife: Plants grown without pesticides can be used to attract animals by providing shelter or food. Butterflies, for instance, need food for the caterpillars (such as snapdragons, nasturtiums, roses) and nectar for the adults (such as columbines, Shasta daisies, purple coneflowers). Hummingbirds need flowers with nectar (such as hollyhocks, sages, fuchsias). Seed-bearing plants left in the garden to develop seeds will attract seed-eating birds such as bushtits and chickadees. A list of commonly grown plants that attract wildlife is given below.

Trees

Alder
Birch
Bottlebrush
Dogwood
European Mountain Ash
Hawthorn
Mulberry
Oak
Sycamore

Shrubs

Arbutus
Barberry
Cotoneaster
Fuschsia
Holly
Mahonia
Pyracantha

Vines

Honeysuckle
Wisteria
Bougainvillea

Low-growing Shrubs or Groundcover

Calluna
Creeping Rosemary
Erica
Iceplant
Sage
Thyme

Section F

SYMBOLS TO USE IN DRAWINGS OF LANDSCAPE PLANS

Top View

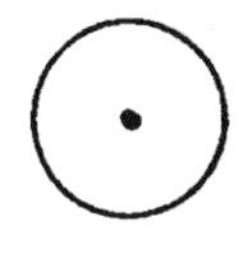

SHRUB

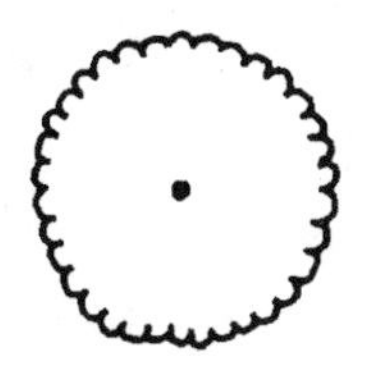

DECIDUOUS OR SHADE TREE

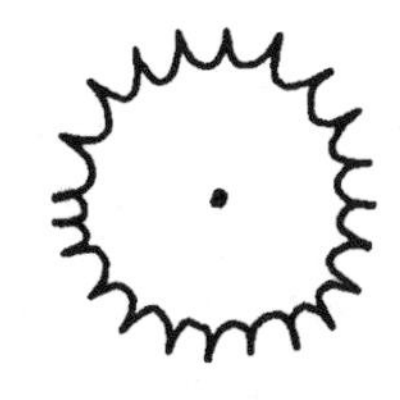

EVERGREEN TREE

GROUNDCOVER

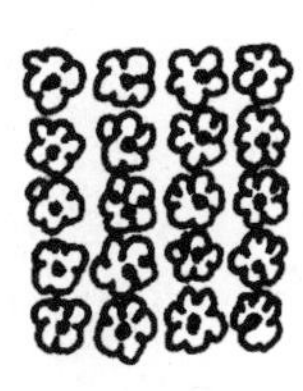

FLOWERS

1 inch = 15 feet

Side View

EVERGREEN

SHADE

ORNAMENTAL

SHRUB

1 inch = 30 feet

Section G

PRINCIPLES OF SUSTAINABLE GARDENING AND LANDSCAPING

The overall principle of sustainable gardening and landscaping is to meet current human needs while protecting and enriching local ecosystems and biodiversity for the future. Sustainable landscapes provide peace, beauty, food, and shelter; through sustainable gardens and landscapes we, in turn, can nurture the earth. We can promote human health, a healthy environment, and help to conserve our most precious resource—biodiversity.

The principles of sustainable gardening and landscaping include using minimal resources and using them efficiently; growing plants that are adapted to the local bioregion and that promote genetic diversity; avoiding chemical additives; and in all ways possible minimizing the impact on natural ecosystems. The methods aim to mimic the local bioregion by being in harmony with local geography, soil conditions, climates, plants, and animals. They nurture and even enhance the natural processes of plant growth, pest management, and soil productivity.

More specifically, the principles of sustainable gardening and landscaping are

- Use minimum amounts of water.
- Use minimum amounts of energy (such as power tools or electricity for water pumps).
- Eliminate or minimize use of chemical fertilizers.
- Eliminate or minimize use of chemical pesticides; use nontoxic methods of pest management instead, including encouraging beneficial animals.
- Eliminate or minimize use of equipment that causes air or noise pollution.
- Recycle garden waste.
- Maximize use of nontoxic, recycled, locally produced garden materials.
- Grow plants appropriate or native to the bioregion (considering soil type and climate).
- To the extent possible, use seeds that promote genetic diversity (nonhybrids and multiple varieties).

- Grow plants and create environments that attract and nurture wildlife.
- Protect topsoil by using appropriate drainage and watering systems.

You will find details about applying these principles in section H. If you do decide to plant a garden or do some landscaping, these are some of the many opportunities and rewards that await you:

- Growing, nurturing, and taking responsibility for living organisms.
- Learning first-hand about the seasons and how all things are interdependent.
- Working with the earth; getting your hands dirty and having fun!
- Growing plants without chemicals.
- Growing your own food.
- Discovering how good "fresh from the garden" food can taste!

Section H

TIPS FOR PLANNING AND MAINTAINING A SUSTAINABLE GARDEN

Here are just a few tips for growing a sustainable garden or landscape. You can find much more information—and information specific to your area—from local experts, books, and other resources.

Healthy top soil, rich in beneficial microorganisms, is vital to any garden. Learn about your soil type, the nutrients it contains or needs, and how well water is absorbed by it. The type of soil you have has a strong influence on how often you need to water:

- Sandy—Sandy soil consists of coarse particles and dries out quickly (too quickly for many plants).
- Clay—Clay soil consists of very dense particles, absorbs water very slowly, and stays wet a long time (too long for many plants).
- Loam—Loam is the best garden mixture. It consists of a mix of particles of different sizes that absorb water easily yet dry out slowly.

Gardeners add amendments to sandy and clay soils to make them more like loam. They also till or dig the soil to lighten and condition it.

Here are some important tips for maintaining healthy soil:

- Compost garden and kitchen waste and use it to amend and mulch garden soil—composting is sometimes called the foundation of sustainable gardening. Compost not only recycles waste, it provides the best source of enrichment for the soil. It supplies beneficial earthworms, fungi, and other microorganisms, as well as a loamy mix of particles to condition garden soil. Organic compost can be purchased if you do not have your own compost. (See Composting later in this section.)
- Fertilize with organic material (compost, manure)—this saves money, time, and prevents toxic runoff.
- Add natural nutrients to soil as needed—most important are the addition of nitrogen (from green manure or compost) and rock phosphorous.
- Mulch around plants—Mulching means covering the soil with organic material such as leaves, bark, wood chips, hay, and compost. Mulching reduces erosion and the loss of moisture from the soil and

keeps weeds from growing. It also protects the soil for the activity of beneficial worms and bacteria and keeps the soil and plant roots cooler in summer and warmer in winter.

- Grow cover crops—Cover crops will enrich the soil in food or other gardens that are replanted each year. Cover crops are quick-growing and have natural bacteria that are able to convert nitrogen in the air into usable nitrogen in the soil. They are grown over the winter and plowed under in the spring. They add organic matter to the soil and provide habitat for beneficial insects, as well as providing nitrogen. Popular cover crops are alfalfa, fava beans, and red clover.
- Rotate crops—Changing from year to year which plants are grown on a piece of land will improve the soil and thereby help keep pests and weeds under control. Although this is particularly important for farmers of larger areas, it will benefit a small garden as well.

Selecting and Placing Plants

Some plants grow best in warm, dry environments; others thrive in cool, moist conditions. Some grow best in sandy soil, others in clay. Choose plants that are appropriate to your soil and climate conditions and that suit your purposes. (See sections E, G, and I for more information on plant choices and types of plants.) In addition:

- If practical, plant a mixture of native and nonnative or edible plants to enhance sustainability and attract wildlife.
- Although you will start with young, small plants or seeds, space plants according to their mature sizes. Plants that are uncrowded are more resistant to pests and diseases. But do not plant them too far apart—plants are good companions for each other in various ways, including providing shade, keeping soil moist, and preventing erosion.
- Plant at the right time of year for your chosen plants—some plants do best when planted in spring, others in fall.

Watering

Sustainable gardens and landscapes use minimum amounts of water by employing planting designs and watering systems that promote efficiency. Some techniques are:

- Grouping—group plants with similar water requirements to make watering efficient.
- Shading—use low-water, larger shrubs or trees to shade other plants. Plants in the shade at least part of the day require less water.
- Planting low-water plants—select plants, shrubs, ground covers, and trees that require less water.
- Use water-saving irrigation systems—efficient systems are drip irrigation and soil soakers. Sprinklers are less efficient because they cause water loss through runoff and evaporation, but where they are needed (for lawns, for instance), use low-output sprinklers with automatic timers.

Using Energy

Sustainable gardening means minimizing the use of all resources, including energy. To minimize energy:

- Use less water—a lot of energy is used to pump water; saving water saves energy.
- Limit use of gas-powered tools—use hand tools instead!
- Plant trees for shade—deciduous trees planted to shade a building will reduce the need for energy for cooling systems in summer.
- Eliminate or minimize use of chemical fertilizers and pesticides—these chemicals are made from petrochemicals, a nonrenewable source of energy.

Managing Pests

Synthetic chemical pesticides can have damaging effects on the environment and on human health. In addition, they kill not only the unwanted insects and other animals but also the beneficial ones. The sustainable alternative most in use today is Integrated Pest Management (IPM). This method uses a combination of least-toxic ways of controlling pests, including

- Physical controls and barriers—There are many physical methods including, for example, hand-picking insects or surrounding the garden with ashes or copper strips as a barrier to snails. Laying traps such as rolls of newspaper to attract earwigs is another type of physical control.

- Cultivation techniques—Keeping plants healthy will ensure fewer pest problems, and keeping gardens clean, well-pruned, and free of weeds will reduce habitat for unwanted animals. Dealing with pests quickly will also reduce the chances of serious pest invasions.
- Biological controls—Introducing a pest's predator is an effective technique—for example, putting ladybugs in the garden to eat aphids.
- Companion planting—Some plants attract certain pests while others repel them. Combining the right plants as companions can be an important pest control. For example, the carrot fly attacks carrots but will not lay its eggs on leeks. The leek moth and onion fly attack leeks but are repelled by carrots. Carrots and leeks are good companions. Many herbs and flowers are also good companions for vegetables.
- Encouraging beneficial animals—Birds, toads, snakes, bats, and other animals are natural insect controllers. Fresh water, bushes for shelter, and food plants will attract birds, for example, which in turn will eat unwanted insects. A Baltimore oriole can eat 17 hairy caterpillars a minute!
- Using safe products—Many products are now available, such as insecticidal soap and herbal repellents that are not poisonous to humans or the environment but are effective against pests. Gardeners can make their own sprays, too, from natural repellents such as garlic, onions, and peppers.

Choosing Garden Materials

To have as little negative impact on the environment as possible, try to use garden materials that are recycled and non toxic. For example, old railroad ties make great borders for raised garden beds. When buying new materials, hunt for those that are made from renewable resources, that are produced locally, and that can be recycled.

Choosing Seeds to Promote Biodiversity

Hybrid seeds, which are most of the seeds available in nurseries and supermarkets, have been bred to produce plants that will grow quickly and be healthy if given the right fertilizers. However, these plants usually will not produce usable seeds. Their seeds either will not grow or

will produce plants with unpredictable and unwanted characteristics. To promote genetic diversity, some gardeners today are using "heirloom seeds" instead, nonhybrid seeds that produce plants whose seeds can be used for future generations. As generation after generation of nonhybrids are grown, they add variety to the gene pool. Gardeners are also finding that these heirloom strains are often more disease-resistant and better tasting than the hybrids. (See Resources section for sources of heirloom seeds.)

If you grow plants from heirloom seeds, you can promote genetic diversity—and save some money while doing it—if you harvest your own seeds for use in following years. Allow some plants to go to seed and collect the most following years. Allow some plants to go to seed and collect the most healthy, mature seeds from several different plants. Dry the seeds completely and store them (in paper bags or glass jars) in a cool, dry place with a constant temperature.

Composting

Composting is basic to sustainable gardening. It is nature's way of recycling—decomposing organic material such as yard clippings, leaves, and kitchen scraps into nutrient-rich organic fertilizer. By recycling such elements as phosphorous, calcium, nitrogen, carbon, and microorganisms, composting helps to maintain the balance of ecosystems. Composting can be done using any of several different processes to encourage decomposition by earthworms, bacteria, fungi, and other organisms. One of the easiest and most popular methods is to build a simple compost pile and add red earthworms as the decomposers.

Section I

GARDEN AND LANDSCAPE DESIGN

People grow gardens and create landscapes for many reasons. Perhaps the most basic reason is our desire to connect with the earth, to establish a closer relationship with the living organisms that sustain us. We grow gardens for food, for flowers, to attract wildlife. We create landscapes for contemplation, recreation, as artistic expression, as memorials to special people or events. There are as many different reasons for gardening and landscaping as there are garden and landscape designs. Throughout history and throughout the world, people have created gardens and landscapes of incredible beauty and variety.

History of Gardens and Landscapes

Historians believe that cultivated gardens were first created in the ancient Persian and Egyptian empires as cool places for rest from the heat of the desert. Their water gardens, using pools and water lilies, are among the oldest forms of gardening. The Romans and, later, cultures in the Middle Ages built gardens inside homes or walls as sanctuaries from the outer world. In the Renaissance, gardens filled with statues became elaborate symbols of wealth and status. The classical French gardens, such as the extensive gardens at the Palace of Versailles, were further developments of the Renaissance styles. These French gardens and landscapes, with their Greek and Roman statues and their rigid formality and control, seem to emphasize people's dominance over nature.

In contrast, Asian gardens developed over the centuries to use winding pathways, spots for rest and contemplation, flowing water, and man-made elements such as bridges or statuary that blend into the landscape. The plantings evoke a tranquil atmosphere. These gardens seem to reflect a balance between people's activities and nature.

For years, much of the landscaping in the United States was patterned after the European styles, especially a style that developed in Great Britain using green lawns and flower borders. This style requires a temperate, wet climate or—if that is not the climate—supplemental water, fertilizer, and probably pesticides. To avoid the need for these

extra resources in the many bioregions in the U.S. that are not temperate and wet, people have been creating regional styles. They have been developing gardens that aim to balance the natural surroundings with the controlled, cultivated areas. These landscapes are more appropriate to local climates, soils, and plant types.

Chaparral gardens in the Southwest and California, luscious shady gardens in the South, flower-filled cottage-type gardens in the Northeast, and cactus gardens in desert areas are a few examples of popular, regional styles.

Three Basic Garden Designs

Designing gardens and landscapes is like painting or building—the designs are limited only by the materials available, the environment, and your imagination. Gardeners might choose a traditional style, or create their own style, combine different styles, or combine different functions for the garden with different styles. Any garden may be "organic" if it is established and maintained without chemical pesticides and fertilizers. Garden designs may be classified into three basic types: plant gardens, food gardens, and habitat gardens. Of course, a garden is often more than one of these types at the same time.

Plant Gardens Many plant gardens are grown for their artistic beauty—for a special combination of colors or forms, for their smells, for variety in textures to see and touch, or for flowers to cut and bring inside. Other plant gardens are designed either to hide or to highlight a building or other structure. Still others are for borders along pathways or to create a quiet resting place. A plant garden may contain only one type of plant—such as a rose garden or rhododendron garden—or it may contain many different species.

A basic tip from landscape designers for creating a pleasing plant garden is to keep the design simple by limiting the number of different plants, clustering plants of similar types together, or choosing plants within a particular color range. Some of the traditional plant garden designs are:

Flower gardens—groupings of flowering plants, including those that live only one season (annuals) and those that last two or more seasons (biennials and perennials). Trees and shrubs are often included in flower garden designs; colors and forms are grouped for contrast and harmony.

Asian gardens—tranquil gardens with soft colors, harmonious groupings of leafy plants (often bamboo or Japanese maples), small bridges, flowing water, and curving pathways. Asian gardens may be shady or in the sun.

English landscapes and gardens—green lawns and borders of flowers and hedges. British cottage-style gardens include mixtures of perennial flowering plants and shrubs (often including roses as well as many other flowers). The color range of these gardens is sometimes limited to create a more balanced look.

Herb gardens—plants grown for their use as medicines or for flavoring foods—such as oregano for Italian tomato sauces, chamomile for stomach-soothing teas, and lavender for fragrances that delight and calm the mind. Herbs are also grown for the color of their leaves—many are striking silver-grays to blue-greens. Traditional herb gardens often feature sundials, beehives, birdbaths, or figurines as focal points.

Rock gardens—natural-looking groupings of rocks with flowering plants, cascading plants, and small shrubs planted among them. Plants may be tucked into cracks or small spaces between rocks. The placement of rocks allows the gardener to include shade-loving plants in cooler spots shaded by the rocks and sun-loving plants in spots where they will be exposed to the sun and to heat from the rocks.

Water gardens—formal or informal pools of water planted with water-loving plants (such as water lilies) and often including a surrounding area of moist ground planted with water-tolerant plants (irises and cattails, for example). Styles vary widely, but water gardens must have plants that will produce oxygen to keep the water clear and support any fish or turtles that may be introduced.

Food Gardens Many people today are growing vegetable gardens. Some grow food in order to have organic produce (grown without chemical fertilizers or pesticides), some to have better tasting and fresher produce, and many for the pure joy of gardening and growing their own vegetables.

Habitat Gardens These gardens are havens for wildlife, designed to attract and meet the needs of birds, beneficial insects, and other living things by providing shelter, space, food, and water. Native plants are

common in habitat gardens because they have evolved in interdependence with the animals in the local ecosystems. Habitat gardens might include plants that provide leaves, fruits, seeds, or nectar as food for animals. Areas with rock crevices or leaf litter or weeds are favored by butterflies and other insects. Diversity of plant species and arrangements is important in habitat gardens in order to attract a variety of animals. Habitat gardeners often include additional features such as birdhouses, bird feeders, butterfly houses, bat boxes, tree limbs or snags, and ponds or birdbaths.

Considerations When Planning a Garden or Landscape

For any type of garden or landscape, gardeners must consider not only their vision and desired purpose for the garden but also the limitations of the climate, the space, and the materials available. Books, magazines, gardening organizations, and services such as agricultural extension offices abound as resources for in-depth advice about garden planning. The following list is a starting point to give you some idea of the things to consider when planning a garden or landscape:

Practical Considerations

- Function of garden (for food, for flowers, to attract wildlife, etc., or a combination of functions)
- Space available
- Existing structures (buildings, walkways, paths that will impact the garden design)
- Water availability and location of source
- Impact on people or ecosystem (allergy considerations, for example, or shading or disturbing neighboring areas)
- Features for special needs such as for disabled people, children, elderly people, or pets
- Cost considerations: cost of building materials (stones, bricks, wood); cost of plants and supplies
- Need for maintenance and cost of maintenance

Ecological Considerations

- Climate (temperature, wind, rainfall, etc.)
- Exposure to sun or shade

- Soil type and condition
- Water flow (drainage patterns)
- Topography—the shape of the land
- Plants native or adapted to local bioregion
- Variety of plants and seeds that promote genetic and species diversity
- Impact on wildlife and environment

Artistic Considerations

- Overall design (formal or informal, traditional or nontraditional, one style or a blend of styles)
- Color
- Smell
- Plant proportions
- Use of nonplant elements (benches, walkways, rocks)

Section J

ORGANIC GARDENING

An organic garden can bring delight in producing the healthiest food possible, beautiful flowers, and glorious herbs. Because organic gardens use materials from living things such as organic soil amendments, pest controls, and fertilizers, they enhance biodiversity without harming the environment.

You may decide to grow an organic garden on your school grounds, in your back yard, or on a vacant lot. Here are eight basic steps for creating and maintaining an organic garden and a guide to creating a seed bank. Be sure to consult books and local experts for more information specific to your area.

Step 1: Divide tasks and responsibilities.

Decide who will be responsible for the various tasks of creating, maintaining, and harvesting your garden. If you are growing a garden at school, much of the growth will take place during the summer. Be sure you can make arrangements to regularly maintain the garden during the summer months.

Step 2: Choose the garden area and develop a detailed plan.

Consider the size of the garden plot, the plants desired, the availability of sunlight and water, and access pathways in the garden. Consider what you want to do with the fruits, vegetables, herbs, or flowers you harvest and choose the right plants for your purposes. For instance, will you want to take the produce home to eat, sell it at a produce stand, donate it to the community, or perhaps share it with your school's food preparers for use in the school cafeteria? To plan for harvests throughout as much of the year as possible, think about your growing seasons and how long different plants take to mature. Plan your planting times and spacings accordingly.

Step 3: Research and obtain garden supplies.

Here is a suggested list of supplies:

Square-nosed spade
Hay or pitch fork
Small trowels

A few feet of chicken wire
String or twine
Garden stakes (or sticks)
Irrigation/watering materials
Organic soil conditioner (compost is best)
Planting soil (for germinating seeds)
Paper cups or transplanting trays
Seeds and/or plants

Step 4: Prepare the soil.

One popular method of preparing garden soil is called "double digging." This method enriches the soil on the top level and breaks up the lower soil so that roots can grow well. Double digging results in garden beds of raised mounds of soil ready for planting.

a. Use the stakes and twine to mark the areas for your garden beds. A good size is 3 feet by 6 feet.
b. If the area is covered with grass, remove it (compost or use it elsewhere). Try to save any topsoil by shaking it off the roots.
c. Dig a trench one spade deep and set the soil to the side. Use the spade or pitchfork and dig down another spade's depth and loosen the soil. Add amendments to the soil in the lower level.
d. Replace the topsoil and dig the next trench right next to it. Move on down the line until the entire bed is "fluffed" or loosened. Be sure to pull out all the old roots, weeds, and rocks as you work the soil.
e. Add a thin layer of soil amendments (compost) across the top of the bed and work it lightly into soil.
f. Repeat for all the beds in the garden.
g. Don't step on the beds after they have been dug or you will pack them down again!

Step 5: Plant plants or seeds.

Determine the appropriate planting times and methods for your plants. To efficiently cover the surface of your garden bed, stagger the spacing of your plants (or seeds) rather than planting them in rows. Use chicken wire to guide your planting of vegetables such as lettuce and other greens, radishes, and carrots. Plant one plant in each chicken-wire hole (or every other hole for larger plants). Seeds can be germinated in the ground or in plastic pots, transplanting trays, or paper cups filled with planting soil.

Moisten the soil before planting seeds or transplanting seedlings. Try to transplant in cool weather or in the evening. When transplanting, dig the hole in the garden soil several inches wider and deeper than the rootmass, rough up the edges of the rootmass, place the plant in the hole, and fill in the hole with a mix of soil and soil amendments. Water the plants in well and don't let them dry out while they are getting established.

Step 6: Water regularly and manage weeds and pests.

Determine your plants' needs for water and establish a watering system and schedule. Check regularly for over- or under-watering. If possible, set up an irrigation system with timers to ensure regular watering. Remove weeds and deal with pests as soon as they are found—this will eliminate more work in the long run. Mulch around plants to reduce weeds and keep the soil moist.

Step 7: Harvest crops and collect seeds.

Because different crops ripen at different times, harvesting is an ongoing process. It's pretty obvious when crops such as tomatoes are ripe and ready to be harvested, but you may have to consult books or experts to determine the right time for harvesting some of your plants. If you allow some plants to go to seed, you can collect their seeds for planting in your garden next year or for storing in a seed bank (see below).

Step 8: Prepare the garden for winter.

Rake up all the old dead plant material and put it in the compost pile. Spread fresh compost and other mulch (fall leaves are great) on top of the garden beds and dig in lightly. Bacteria and other organisms can then decompose the compost further and the eggs, larvae, and pupae of unwanted insects will be exposed to winter cold and birds. You might also want to prepare the soil of a small area to be ready for planting early spring crops such as peas and spinach. Preparing the bed before winter avoids having to dig in the wet soil of early spring.

Creating a Seed Bank

If you have grown nonhybrid plants (see "Choosing Seeds to Promote Biodiversity" in section H), you may want to harvest seeds and save them in a seed bank for your own use later and to contribute to genetic diversity.

a. Allow some plants to go to seed. Collect seeds from several different plants, choosing the seeds that look healthy and mature.
b. Dry the seeds completely.
c. Research the different storage needs of specific seeds. Most seeds will last well for one year in paper bags. For longer storage, most need to be sealed well in glass jars. Beans and peas, however, require air and must always be stored in paper bags.
d. Store the seeds in a cool, dry place with a constant temperature. Both heat and humidity must be avoided, but most seeds will not be harmed by temperatures below freezing.
e. Establish a simple and accurate method for organizing the seeds in your seed bank. Label containers with contents and dates and maintain a record or catalog of all the seeds.

GLOSSARY

biodiversity The variety of living things on earth.

biome A major regional or global biotic community, such as a grassland or desert, characterized by the main forms of plant life and the prevailing climate.

bioregion A smaller part of a biome characterized by plant life and climate but also taking into account geography, waterways, and other special features.

chaparral A biome characterized by hot, dry summers and cool, moist winters and dominated by a dense growth of mostly small-leaved evergreen shrubs.

climate The meteorological conditions, including temperature, precipitation, and wind, that characteristically prevail in a particular region.

coniferous Needle-leaved or scale-leaved, chiefly evergreen, cone-bearing trees or shrubs such as pines, spruces, and firs.

deciduous Falling off or shed at a specific season or stage of growth; shedding or losing foliage at the end of the growing season.

ecosystem An ecological community together with its environment, functioning as a unit.

extinction The fact or condition of ceasing to exist.

genetic Of or relating to genetics or genes.

habitat The area or type of environment in which an organism or ecological community normally lives or is found.

interdependence Mutual dependence.

irrigation To supply dry land with water by means of ditches, pipes, or streams; water artificially; to make fertile or vital as if by watering.

landscape (v.) To adorn or improve a section of ground by contouring and by planting flowers, shrubs, or trees.

pesticide A chemical used to kill pests, especially insects.

precipitation Any form of water, such as rain, snow, sleet, or hail, that falls to the earth's surface.

savanna A flat grassland of tropical or subtropical regions.

species A basic category of related organisms capable of interbreeding; an organism belonging to such a category.

taiga A subarctic, evergreen coniferous forest of northern Eurasia located just south of the tundra and dominated by firs and spruces.

temperate Characterized by moderate temperatures, weather, or climate; neither hot nor cold.

topsoil The upper part of the soil.

tropical Of, occurring in, or characteristic of the Tropics; hot and humid.

tundra A treeless area between the icecap and the tree line of Arctic regions, having a permanently frozen subsoil and supporting low-growing vegetation such as lichens, mosses, and stunted shrubs.